a VICTORY GARDEN *for* TRYING TIMES

a VICTORY GARDEN *for* TRYING TIMES

a memoir

DEBI GOODWIN

DUNDURN
TORONTO

Cover image: shutterstock.com/annarepp
Printer: Webcom, a division of Marquis Printing Inc.

Library and Archives Canada Cataloguing in Publication

Title: A victory garden for trying times : a memoir / Debi Goodwin.
Names: Goodwin, Debi, author.
Identifiers: Canadiana (print) 20190119497 | Canadiana (ebook) 2019011956X | ISBN 9781459745056 (softcover) | ISBN 9781459745063 (PDF) | ISBN 9781459745070 (EPUB)
Subjects: LCSH: Goodwin, Debi. | LCSH: Goodwin, Debi—Family. | LCSH: Cancer—Patients—Family relationships. | LCSH: Gardening—Psychological aspects. | LCSH: Gardens—Psychological aspects. | LCSH: Grief. | LCSH: Widows—Biography. | LCGFT: Autobiographies.
Classification: LCC SB454 .G66 2019 | DDC 635.092—dc23

1 2 3 4 5   23 22 21 20 19

We acknowledge the support of the **Canada Council for the Arts**, which last year invested $153 million to bring the arts to Canadians throughout the country, and the **Ontario Arts Council** for our publishing program. We also acknowledge the financial support of the **Government of Ontario**, through the **Ontario Book Publishing Tax Credit** and **Ontario Creates**, and the **Government of Canada**.

Nous remercions le **Conseil des arts du Canada** de son soutien. L'an dernier, le Conseil a investi 153 millions de dollars pour mettre de l'art dans la vie des Canadiennes et des Canadiens de tout le pays.

Care has been taken to trace the ownership of copyright material used in this book. The author and the publisher welcome any information enabling them to rectify any references or credits in subsequent editions.

The publisher is not responsible for websites or their content unless they are owned by the publisher.

Printed and bound in Canada.

VISIT US AT

 dundurn.com |  @dundurnpress | dundurnpress | dundurnpress

Dundurn
3 Church Street, Suite 500
Toronto, Ontario, Canada
M5E 1M2

For Peter

Chapter One

BEFORE WINTER COMES each year, I plant my garlic. In late October, usually. Early enough to give the thread-thin roots time to poke out of each clove and anchor in the soil before the first hard frost stiffens the ground, but late enough so sprouts as delicately green as fresh peas won't prematurely shoot out of the earth on warm days only to be destroyed when the killing weather descends. That year, though, I waited until November because the fall was warm. Unusually warm. And I was worn out with worry, my routines as off-kilter as climate-change weather.

Planting any kind of vegetable — a seed, a seedling, a clove — is an act of faith: Faith that there will be enough sun, enough rain. That disease, insects, and blight can be kept at bay long enough for beets to fatten in the soil, tomatoes to turn red and sweet, beans to multiply on poles. That we will be there to harvest them. But planting garlic in the fall, expecting it to survive the winter underground and then to start transmuting one clove into a head of new cloves at the exact right time, takes a special kind of faith. Plucking fat new heads from the ground eight or nine months later is a special kind of victory.

By the time I planted that fall, I'd had my garlic ready to go for weeks: five organic varieties from the local farmers' market and a few heads left over from my crop of the past summer. I'd pulled the individual cloves from the heads, careful to leave as much of the papery protective cover around each clove as I could, and then I stored them in a basket in the cold cellar until it was time. "Plant them during the full moon," a farmer at the market had told me in a low, gruff voice, as if he were sharing a secret. I missed one full moon but didn't want to wait for another. I assumed freezing weather was on its way even in the town of Niagara-on-the-Lake, in one of the warmest zones in Ontario, where I then lived. And I wanted the garden put to bed for the year because there were more urgent things to do.

By the time I set out to plant my garlic, we'd received a definitive diagnosis for my husband, Peter: third-stage cancer of the esophagus.

The diagnosis came after a short holiday to celebrate my sixty-fifth birthday that fall, a trip to Colorado and beautiful New Mexico, where our faces glowed in the afternoon light and our thoughts grew darker over Peter's increasing inability to swallow and therefore eat. In the almost twenty-seven years we'd been together, Peter had faced many physical challenges and conquered them all. We thought this was just another bump in a history of bad luck with his health. Maybe we shouldn't have gone on that trip, but doctors had told us that Peter's difficulties with swallowing could be anything and that swallowing problems are common as we age. We had finally made it to the specialist, a gastroenterologist in St. Catharines, the day before our departure. "Go on your holiday," he'd said. Neither he nor anyone else had said the C-word about what seemed to be a polyp seen on an X-ray, and we were all too willing to accept their lack of concern. Blindly, I suppose.

Peter had found me the highest sand dune in North America to climb and he was eager to finally visit Santa Fe. I thrilled at exploring natural wonders, especially empty canyons, open deserts, and dunes, while Peter was content to sit and admire them. He was eager to learn the peculiarities of a new city — its odd museums, its quirky characters, and its unique past — while I loved to photograph its architecture, its splashes of colour and personality. I didn't want to give up my birthday trip. Peter didn't want to ruin another of my significant birthdays with a medical crisis, as had happened before. It was just for two weeks, after all. So, we went.

As soon as we got back, Peter underwent a probe and a biopsy that he'd scheduled before we left. After that procedure Peter had to follow up with the gastroenterologist's office for an appointment. He was given a time two weeks later, a routine appointment. And we took that as a good sign. There was nothing urgent; this was something *routine*.

But when we arrived for the appointment, we sat in the crowded waiting room, nervous, afraid of what we might hear. When the doctor, a short, grey-haired man, called us into his office, we followed him into a small, claustrophobic room with a desk in the centre. I sensed there was clutter all around me, on file cabinets, on the desk, on the walls, but they were all in my periphery; I was focused on that doctor and what he'd say. Peter introduced me as his wife but the doctor didn't respond, didn't even look at me. Peter and I sat down in the two chairs across from him and watched as he shuffled papers. Without a glance at us, he turned his face toward his computer screen and muttered, "It's cancer."

Peter and I stared at the doctor in disbelief, waiting for something else from him, some hint of reassurance. I had to ask him what kind of cancer.

"Cancer of the esophagus," he replied, not returning my gaze.

"How can we get treatment quickly?" I asked.

"You can't," he said in a way that hit me like a snarl. "This is Ontario. There are procedures."

We left his office with a form for blood work and little confidence that this doctor had a plan. In the hallway, Peter and I hugged silently. On the way home, we stopped the car and called my daughter.

"But is it really cancer?" Jane asked.

Like me, Jane had come to think of Peter as invincible. He'd been told he had cancer before. Twice. Once, an internist, after seeing a mass on Peter's X-ray, had operated for colon cancer only to discover Peter's appendix had burst and the mass was dead tissue. Another time I had to rush Peter to hospital when a blood test revealed a hemoglobin count so low most people would have been dead. The first doctors we encountered that time were certain Peter had leukemia, but a clever hematologist diagnosed his inability to absorb B12 as the problem, and monthly injections of the vitamin brought back Peter's vitality. But Peter and I both sensed that this time was different, and we told Jane so.

"But Petey will beat it," Jane said of the father figure she had known since she was three. "He always does."

I didn't say anything; I wondered how much damage one body could take.

At home, Peter and I cried and tried to figure out how we could make things happen. We were journalists, competent people. We knew how to put things into action. We would find the best doctor in Toronto, get a reference somehow. It was an appeal to our family doctor that got us into the well-respected Juravinski Cancer Centre in Hamilton the next week. There, we met a team of oncologists who were kind, efficient, and ready to tackle the cancer immediately. In an examining room, the lead oncologist drew a picture on the paper sheet on the bed that showed the tumour in the middle of Peter's esophagus, and he took the time to describe the tumour with terms like *squamous cell carcinoma*. The word *squamous* sounded like *squash* to me, but he told us these cells were the flat cells that lined the esophagus and they were now cancerous in the location of the tumour. He talked about treatments and didn't mince his words when it came to his anger over the slowness of the specialist in St. Catharines. And we knew we were in good hands.

In the following weeks, a CT scan and a PET scan revealed that Peter's tumour had spread into the surrounding lymph glands, making the cancer Stage 3. But there was still so much to learn: Could the tumour be excised after radiation and chemo-therapy treatments? Would the chemotherapy destroy the stray cancer? Had the PET scan missed spots of cancer in other parts of his body?

In my garden, I knelt on the cold ground, drew lines with a stick, dug small holes six inches apart, and dropped a garlic clove in each hole. The solitary cloves looked so pale, so small, so fragile in the cold earth. What chance did they or any of us have? I patted the soil over the point of each clove with little of the joy I usually felt at the moment I set the process of growth into motion. I couldn't help wondering if Peter would be there to savour our late-summer favourite: bruschetta made with top-pings from my garden, including fresh, finely chopped garlic. Rain began to fall on the earth. Planting my garlic that fall took all the faith I had.

That winter, we were supposed to go somewhere warm; we had a guest house booked overlooking the sacred waters of the Ganges River and an apartment we could settle into for weeks in laid-back Goa, and there was a chance I could swing a press visit to a towering hotel that resembled a windblown sailboat on the edge of Dubai. It was how we would spend our third winter of semi-retirement. It was how it was supposed to be.

Each day in November and into December our fingers hesitated over the computer keys, not wanting to hit the buttons to cancel the flight booked on points, the apartment carefully chosen, the guest house with the view. But by mid-December we had. Each day of January we knew where we should have been: drinking coffee in the Burj Al Arab hotel, dining in the desert under a Bedouin tent, chanting no to the touts of Varanasi. Each day in February we wondered what we would have been cooking and reading in our small Indian rooms. Not with rancour, but with the detached wistfulness of imagining someone else's day.

But that winter, we were home. When we weren't out looking for answers. When we weren't driving the hour from Niagara-on-the-Lake to Hamilton for daily radiation and weekly chemo. When we weren't waiting anxiously for weeks after the treatments to see if surgery was possible.

We gave up going to movies and large social events where Peter might catch a cold that could prove truly dangerous to someone whose immune system had been suppressed by chemotherapy. We did go on one outing: to a historic house up for auction on the Niagara River. Whenever we'd looked at houses in the past, I would imagine a life in every one and tell Peter where each piece of furniture could go. As we left, he'd say, "So, should we put in an offer?" and I would usually answer, "No," with a list of the drawbacks of the property. It drove him crazy. But on that day, we both played the game. The old house needed extensive renovations and had bedrooms on the second floor, which we'd always ruled out for our retirement years. Yet we wandered through the oversized house, deciding where our offices and a new kitchen would be. We never made an offer; we both knew that the house was a complete fantasy, but it was one we needed on a fearful winter day.

I've always leaned toward hibernation in winter; that year I bordered on becoming a hermit. Among the feel-better aphorisms on Facebook there was one that rang true to me during those dark months: "The answer to loneliness is solitude." I've known that ever since I was a small child disappearing into the orchard of my family farm to get away from all the noisy, busy people who had little time for me. Then, I built forts in the dirt, felt safe sitting among the trees and vegetables. As an adult, I had to have a reason to be in the dirt. A passion for gardening became my excuse, my escape, my therapy.

When I'm angry, weeds in my garden don't have a chance. I pull out those suckers the way boxers hit punching bags, with all my force and a clenched face. A single weed can represent the whole universe or one person: the ex, a boss, anyone I feel has done me wrong. And once that weed is out of the ground and wilting in a basket, some of the powerlessness along with the fear and the insecurities that created my anger dry up, too. And I can sit on the ground calm enough to find perspective and a way forward. When I'm less angry, just mildly annoyed, I deadhead plants, cutting off the dried flowers so new ones will grow. When I'm sad, I contemplate the garden, letting its curves, its textures, its colours soothe me like a warm bath. When I'm happy — and that happens frequently in the garden — I pick vegetables, herbs, and flowers to bring into the house along with my joy. To nurture myself and others.

In the space of a year in our new house, I'd come to know its garden more intimately than the sunspots on my arms. The previous owners had spent sixteen years turning a double lot into a garden with flowering trees, sculpted shrubs, rose bushes, hydrangeas, rhododendrons, and one of the most glorious flowering dogwood trees in town. It was too fussy a garden for my taste, so slowly I'd changed each bed to suit me, to transform this highly managed garden into something that felt like my own. As I worked, I came to know the needs of each inch of the garden — where the purslane, the knotweed, and the clover leaves of the yellow wood sorrel would burst through the soil; where plants would wither most quickly in the dry spells; where I had to move perennials to give others extra space.

We had a few overarching principles for the redesign: Peter and I both wanted more trees, especially evergreens to naturally fence the limits of our two-hundred-foot-deep lot. I wanted more rocks everywhere, having left behind in Toronto a garden filled with twenty years' worth of rock collecting. But above all else, I wanted more food from the garden. I wanted fruit trees, a dedicated herb garden, and larger plots for vegetables. In the first full summer, I dug up a flower garden to create a second vegetable patch for the following year and chose locations for more trees and berry bushes. All I had to do was wait for the next spring.

In December, the lawn was still a vibrant green, the kale producing new shoots. Every time I looked out the window, I had the illusion that I could get back to the garden any day. El Niño was with us that winter, and a sharpened awareness of the real threat of climate change. While I welcomed the clear roads on our daily drives to Hamilton, others found the lack of snow in the early winter creepy, another sign the world, so tense over terrorist attacks and the flood of refugees from the war in Syria, was out of control. The state of the Canadian economy didn't help the mood much. While we appreciated the cheap price of gas, we fretted over falling commodity markets and the darkening financial outlook for our country. And as our loonie dove lower against the American greenback, we bemoaned eight-dollar cauliflowers and spotted green beans at five dollars a pound. In the back of my mind, past the worry, an idea seeded that I would increase the amount of organic vegetables I grew as a way to cope with the world's trying times and to do my bit for the planet.

If it had been any other season — spring, summer, or fall — I would have been out in the garden for hours each day pulling weeds, trimming, digging, watering, whatever needed doing, whatever soothed me. And I would have ended the day so tired I could have slept.

But that winter, when I couldn't dig in the garden, I needed something else to do to quiet my mind. I'd given up sessional teaching because of its restrictions. I'd spent the previous winter painting rooms in colours called Elephant's Breath, Smoked Trout, and Paul Revere Pewter, and I'd arranged all the fixes to our new home so we'd be free to write and travel now. We felt we'd earned that breathing space in our lives. Peter certainly had.

Chronic pain had clung to him. His story of medical trauma had started when he was just an infant who contracted polio; it had led to a lifetime of mobility issues, including one year in a body cast. In a bed. As an adolescent. Surgery three years before his cancer diagnosis had repaired much of the damage to his left leg and hip and had left him pain-free for the first time in his life — he just woke up and the pain was gone. It was our time to savour what we'd accomplished.

We'd started a blog together called *The Third Phase* to document life after work and the issues of aging. What had we done wrong to have this phase snatched away so quickly? Expected too much? Loved each other too much? What the frigging fuck?

With our schedule so full of medical appointments, I doubted I'd ever find the focus to write anything good again. So, I joined a group to sponsor a Syrian refugee family. I signed up for a photography course. Anything to fill in the gaps between treatments, to decrease the hours of waiting and fear. But they were not enough. Nothing was enough to plaster over the hole in my heart. Mostly, I ended up spending mindless hours playing Mah-Jong on my iPad.

We both sought comfort in routine. Each morning, I walked down the half flight of stairs from our bedroom to find Peter at his desk already working at his computer, my heart skipping to see him still there.

"So," he'd say, and then immediately begin to explain some new detail he'd learned about the expansion of the universe, our provincial government's contempt for unions, or the closing of the last school in town. You just never knew.

Even if Peter had brought me a coffee in bed, as he often did, I'd sidestep toward the kitchen, craving a second cup before I could face the encyclopedia of his brain.

When we'd first spotted our house online, I'd known immediately where Peter's office would be. We'd had a wall built with pocket doors to create a room in the cavernous space off the entry, and I'd arranged the dark oak bookshelves from his old office to wrap around the walls. He'd picked out a desk that had an insert in the front for more books. My first view as I came downstairs those mornings was Peter in his womb of books.

"You can never have too many books," he'd say to anyone who didn't understand his need to be surrounded by knowledge and language. Who didn't understand that for the bedridden, other people's adventures and stories of easy movements in the world freed a mind from the confines of one's own.

Each morning, once I had my second coffee in hand, I headed to my office at the back of the house, with its pale maple furnishings gathered from rooms in our old house. I stared at the photos on my desk as the computer booted up. Jane at five on a ferry to Manitoulin Island, strands of red hair flying above her head in the wind, her eyes screwed tight in pure joy. Peter on a trip to Turkey, handsome and pensive as he contemplated something in the distance he'd make a note about to research later. These were my peeps, the people who'd given me some of my life's sweetest moments: the three of us on the L-shaped couch in the old house watching a movie from Blockbuster with Schmidt the schnauzer curled up at our feet; Peter and Jane on a snowy Sunday intent on a Lord of the Rings marathon — director's cut; Peter laughing with his whole body at a poem Jane wrote him for Christmas morning; Peter sipping grappa at Florian's in St. Mark's Square as the orchestra played and the cool night air of Venice caressed our bare arms; Jane and Peter negotiating their relationship when he came into her life (she to be the only person in the whole wide world allowed to call him Pete or Petey, he the only one who could call her kid); me driving them on the interstate to visit our friends A and D in New York while I pretended to be in the chorus of Bruce Springsteen's "Rocky Ground" and they were my silent audience; Peter's bread; Peter's rice and beans; Peter's mashed potatoes pounded into smooth submission with his remarkable upper-body strength we assumed he'd inherited from his stevedore grandfather; the hugs of those strong arms. How could I ever exist without either Peter or Jane? What would I even be?

I quickly looked away from the photographs, typed in my password, and waited. The new house was quiet, always quiet. But what if the silence I loved went on and on? What if Peter's mellifluous voice — a storyteller's voice, a voice that still thrilled me with endearments — stopped reverberating in this house? I fingered one of the small rocks on my desk that I'd found in the southwest, the one shaped like a heart with a crack that ran down its side.

Then, instead of attempting to write, I hunched over the keyboard and searched the internet for causes of esophageal cancer and survival rates, the browser's memory filling in the words after the first letters I tapped. Nothing answered my questions; nothing gave me any assurance Peter would make it out alive. It was nothing but an exercise of masochism in the morning.

At some point, I must have started searching food sites, perhaps for a list of ingredients that combat cancer. I did that a lot. I don't recall how, but I found myself suddenly staring at an archival plan for a Victory Garden, the type of garden so heavily promoted on two continents during two world wars to push anyone with a plot of dirt to grow their own vegetables. But it was like magic when I did. What I knew about Victory Gardens then was they were about hope, about fighting back against enemies trying to take away what you had. Outside my window, the vegetable patch lay dormant under a layer of straw to keep down the weeds over the winter. But in my head, I could see it thriving. I could see myself walking between the rows, tying a tomato plant to a pole here, thinning the new beets there, pulling a weed now and again. And I could see Peter in that picture. Not in the garden. The garden was my domain. But I could see him in the yard. See a future there with both of us in it. Is that how victories come? By imagining them first?

The map was a legal-sized piece of paper, sepia coloured. From the Second World War. American. On twenty-nine lines, it listed the vegetables needed to sustain a family of five for a year on a plot of land twenty-five feet by fifty feet. Vegetables I'd eaten as a child like potatoes, green beans, and tomatoes shared space with lima beans, collard greens, and rutabagas, relics of my grandmother's era. Although the vegetables were just names, I could picture each one, see its wholeness, smell its freshness, taste its hope. My garden would be different. There'd be kale, squash, and arugula with the beets, beans, and tomatoes, and more if I could squeeze them in. It was bounty I wanted, proof of life in my own backyard. A Victory Garden over the fear that cancer had brought into our home. A Victory Garden for trying times.

With a tingle of excitement in my fingers, I searched for nursery sites, videos of Midwest farmers planting in the forties, methods for improving my soil. As my own Victory Garden took shape in my mind, it wasn't joy I felt, but the possibility there could be joy again.

I jumped from my chair with an energy I hadn't had in weeks. The casters pushed up the silk Indian carpet but I didn't stop to smooth it down.

"Yo, Pete," I yelled. "Wanna whooping?" It was our code for a break and a game of backgammon at the dining table in the great room. No one else used our code; no one else ever would. In our Toronto house, we'd both chuckled when one of us had yelled the challenge outside, wondering what the neighbours would think.

Peter had taught me to play backgammon in the first few months of our connection. In his walk-up apartment. With our clothes back on. I went on to be the player who won most often, something that delighted him. He kept score wherever we travelled and had yet to find a country he could win in, a story he loved to tell. *A* for Argentina was off the list. So was *E* for England, *F* for France. And *I* for Italy and India. *T* for Turkey and *V* for Vietnam and so on. But we still had so much of the alphabet to go.

As he walked to the table with a slight hitch to his gait and the familiar click of his cane, which he was using less and less, I said, "I think I have a project."

I told him about the Victory Garden. And he nodded. Pleased.

He always told visitors that he was feeling fine, that this "cancer thing" was harder on me than on him. I knew he didn't like to be a burden, but I still found the comment strange. He was the one facing his mortality. What was I facing? I gave it as little thought as I could. Perhaps I kept the truth hidden like furballs, one in my throat and one in the bottom of my gut.

For now, there was the planning of a Victory Garden to fill the cold hours of winter. I threw the dice on the wooden board with a clack. There were seed catalogues to get, measuring to do, nutritional needs of plants to be learned.

"That'll be great," he said, throwing his own dice. He began to talk books, a blog, the drone he'd buy to photograph the garden's growth. But I wasn't really listening. My head was already past the great room's wall of windows, in the garden the next summer, coaxing my tomatoes and cutting chard while Peter sat on the deck, watching me and learning new things.

Chapter Two

I SUSPECT PETER RECOGNIZED how perfectly this project suited me before I did, in that way a true partner sees the other and their needs so clearly. It was one of the things I loved about him and had come to depend on.

A Victory Garden *was* the perfect project for me, especially now that I lived in the Niagara Region, an area so connected to my past.

I'd grown up with my parents and three siblings on a small fruit farm — about thirty acres — in Grimsby, Ontario, a town located between Hamilton and Niagara Falls. The farm rested below the escarpment on an old seabed, where the receding waters had left behind rich soil that was especially fertile for fruits like peaches. From my bedroom window, I could see Lake Ontario beyond the rows of trees and, on a clear day, across the lake to Toronto and the tall buildings that grew up there as I grew from a toddler with a teepee and a rocking horse in my room to a teenager in a miniskirt listening to the Beatles, wanting to be elsewhere. Since my father was the principal of the only high school in town, I had a greater incentive to leave than most. And, like many a farm kid, I longed, through my school years, to get to the city where I thought my life would truly start, without realizing how much the red-brick Victorian house with the white lace woodwork that I grew up in and the orchards that came with it would stay with me.

My parents rented the land from my maternal grandparents, who'd received the house and the orchard from a man who owed them money. The story goes that the man was on his way to debtors' prison, but since he liked my grandfather, he settled one of his debts with that land. It's a strange Dickensian kind of story, I know, but anyone who could explain it to me is long gone.

Orchards were in my mother's blood; she was descended from seven generations of Niagara landowners, the first of which had settled in the region after families loyal to the British Crown had fled their homes during the American Revolution and received as their reward land grants on what was then British land.

But it was my father who put his heart into the soil, giving his summers — free from his job as a teacher and, later, high-school principal — to tilling, fertilizing, and harvesting. In the evenings, he would tend his vegetable garden, a patch in among the cherry trees that he'd cleared to grow enough produce to feed our family, not just in the summer months, but until the next seeds could be planted.

I loved being out in the garden with my father on spring evenings when the golden light stayed strong until my early bedtime, when the only sounds were the barking of dogs and slamming of screen doors in the distance. My father taught me how to use the hoe to gently break up the soil between the rows and how to set the small plants into holes and pat the spring-cold earth around them. As the days grew longer I rushed to the garden after school to feel how the sun had warmed the soil and see how much taller the plants were. In the late summer and fall, I shared my father's pride in picking the first beans, the first tomatoes, the first squash, and carrying them into the kitchen to my mother. My father didn't talk much as we worked, but in his companionship in the garden, in his desire to feed us all, I felt his love more than anywhere else.

Both my parents had expectations of me as a girl born in the fifties. I felt my mother's more strongly. "Why can't you be like T?" she'd say, comparing me to a cousin who always looked neat and clean, who smiled and didn't shy away from talking politely with adults in her sweet voice. In other words, my antithesis. I knew I didn't want to be like T, but the admonitions always left me wondering what I did want to be. My father never voiced the same concerns as my mother, but neither did he disagree with them. But in the garden, working beside him, none of that mattered. What I became could wait for later.

On winter evenings, my father passed his time dog-earing pages in the Stokes seed catalogue, circling pictures of some vegetables, crossing out others, and filling out forms. I never saw myself becoming like him in that way. Through my working and parenting years there was simply no time. A quick visit to garden centres for plants was all I could manage. And in retirement, the master plan was never supposed to involve cold Canadian nights waiting for spring. Peter and I planned to find a cheap and warm country each winter where we'd spend our evenings reading about what sights or markets we'd visit the next day.

But as the early darkness filled our house in the months of Peter's cancer treatments, when all travel plans were off the books, I finally got that, for my father, imagining the garden, deciding what varieties of vegetables he'd grow, fed his optimism for the future. Helped him through the winter. My father has been dead for more than two decades, but I felt he, like Peter, would be cheering on my project.

Both my parents came to adulthood in a depression and then started their marriage during a war when my father left teaching to train Royal Air Force pilots how to navigate in planes. As a couple, they knew how to scrimp. The vegetables from my father's garden that could be frozen were packed away in the freezer; those that could be canned were boiled in Mason jars; those that could sit out the winter were stored in bushel baskets and boxes of sand in a cobwebby, dark, and dank room in the back of the basement. My parents understood sustainability long before the word was cool. I never heard them speak about the concept of the Victory Garden, but they certainly lived by its intent, understood its inspiration.

And that intent seeped into me. After my father's death, I started growing vegetables in my small urban garden. For years, I dug with his shovels and supported my tomatoes with his slowly rusting stakes. And for years after my mother's death, I kept Mason jars filled with her stewed tomatoes, my favourite comfort food of all time. I remember standing next to her at the kitchen sink, peeling tomatoes from my father's garden and stuffing them into glass jars along with a little salt and onion before she'd set the sealed jars in big blue aluminum pots on the stove. On winter evenings, we'd have a bowl of those tomatoes to start the meal. Even after we all left home, my mother bottled so many tomatoes, all her children had a winter's supply.

As I entered the working world, first as a teacher, I looked forward to those tomatoes after a bad day. A few years after my mother's death, I finally had to open the last jars I'd stored in my basement and dump out the contents, the fear of botulism becoming greater than my desire for nostalgia's taste. My past was in those jars. I might have the sap of fruit trees in my veins, but my memory muscles have been nurtured by homegrown vegetables.

Peter also knew that losing myself in the garden was my kind of meditation. I think all gardeners are loners at heart who seek solitude and contemplation by working in the dirt. And just as I knew he needed his alone time with his books, he knew I needed time when nothing else mattered to me but the work I was doing in the garden.

I put my need for solitude and my ingrained feelings of being a loner down to my earliest summers on the family farm. After my parents took over the care of the land, their summer days were filled with constant trips between the house and the barn, the house and the orchard. I know because I watched them go back and forth. My parents moved to the farm when my siblings were old enough to roam on their own, anywhere they wanted on the property and beyond. My two brothers had the greatest freedom; they explored the escarpment that loomed just across the highway, nearby creeks, and the town of Grimsby. But I was the baby, the youngest by nearly five years, and during our first summers at that house, I was too young to be let loose and my sister not old enough to be entrusted with my care. My parents' solution wasn't intended to be cruel. But on a farm and before daycare, their options were limited. My father fenced off the side yard, creating a giant playpen where I could be left when my mother couldn't be with me, where I'd be safe from trucks backing up, the tractor turning into the barn with a dray loaded with baskets of peaches, and the strangers who came to pick the fruit or to buy it.

One of my brothers still likes to tease me about how I spent my time in the pen standing by the gate looking out even though I had a whole yard to play in behind me. I suspect I wasn't in that pen as often as I imagine and I don't remember much of my time there. I know I played under a spreading lilac tree in the corner closest to the gate. And I remember digging in the soil beneath the tree while keeping an eye out for movement.

That's why I believe my sense of never truly being a part of something came from those summer days. From watching through the gate as others passed by. But, perhaps, I also gained from that time my love of solitude, my need to creep away and feel the dirt on my hands.

Once I was old enough to be freed, I snuck across the highway to an ice cream stand, with coins plundered from the cash box in the kitchen, and treated friends I was trying to win over. The stand sold vanilla ice cream, prewrapped in paper, and plopped into sugar cones. After we ate our cones, we climbed the escarpment in search of salamanders we could keep in jars. I travelled as far as a young girl in a small town could. But wherever I went, however I spent my free summer days, there'd be a point in the afternoon where I'd have to get to a tree in the orchard or crawl under my bed to be alone. That has stayed with me in my need for places where I can hide out and find resilience in the earth and its seasons.

As an adult, I became a haphazard gardener. Work, a first failed marriage, single parenthood, and my new family with Peter commanded my time. I had a garden whenever I had a backyard, but it was always a hobby, part of keeping a house looking as *Better Homes and Gardens* as I could. It was only after my mother died one spring, when I was in my forties, that I truly reconnected with that intense need to sort through my emotions in the act of digging. In the days following her death, I wanted nothing more than to be alone, and I found nowhere better to be alone than on the "reverse ravine" of the home Peter and I had purchased in Toronto.

I had been slowly bringing the hill back to life after the former homeowner's neglect. Neighbours told us the woman had come from the West and had cut down all the trees to make the hill look like a prairie. Weeds and junk trees had taken over the empty land. I planted pachysandra and ivy on the slopes, cedars and pine trees on level ground reinforced with walls of timber. By the fifth year of our ownership, I had one large swath of weeds and eroding soil left to contend with; its enhancement was going to be my summer project. But in the days between my mother's death and her funeral, I disappeared into the patch, pulled out every weed, reshaped the space with rocks and timbers. Prepared it for new plantings. And I came to remember how solitude and silence had always been balms to me. In those few days on my hill, I felt that solitude, silence, and a scrap of land to whip into shape were nothing short of heaven. Now, I wondered if I could find that peace again out in my Victory Garden in the months ahead.

Chapter Three

IT WAS HARD TO KEEP HOPE ALIVE or imagine any kind of victory in the early winter that year. Through the month of December and into January, Peter had his daily radiation treatments to shrink the tumour in his esophagus to a size that could be cut out. In the best-case scenario, the radiation would necrotize the tumour and destroy the cancerous cells that had reached beyond the esophagus. That's what I wanted. To see the invaders dead. Our days were built around the drive to Hamilton. On radiation days, I barely had time to park before Peter would text me to come back and pick him up.

The team of doctors at the Juravinski Cancer Centre had given us two options for Peter's treatment. One involved twenty-five rounds of targeted radiation along with five chemotherapy sessions to support the radiation's work so surgery would be possible. The other involved months of chemotherapy. Peter and I both agreed with the doctors' assessment that, because of Peter's history of blood problems, the first option would be the best. And we both wanted the cancer out of his body as fast as possible.

Reading the literature about treatments was a depressing affair. The list of side effects Peter could experience from chemotherapy alone — nausea, anemia, hair loss, memory changes, swelling that could send him to the emergency room — was frightening. And I couldn't help wondering what lasting damage those drugs would do to Peter's body once the cancer was gone. But, as in any war, you fight the enemy by the means you have and think about the consequences later.

There was one warning, though, that forced me to realize just how poisonous the drugs being pumped into Peter's body were. The nurses told Peter that whenever he went to the bathroom in the days following chemo, he was to sit on the toilet even if he was just urinating so that no spray could escape into the air. Then, he had to flush the toilet twice with the lid down so that no traces of the drugs could irritate his skin or cause harm to any other person. And that fluid was coursing through his body.

Peter suffered few of the outward signs of chemotherapy damage, but his oncologist did have to cancel treatments twice because Peter's white blood count was too low. Despite our awareness of the toxicity of the chemo drugs, we both felt cheated, fearful three treatments wouldn't be enough to give the radiation the boost it needed, even though the oncologist didn't seem worried. We wanted all the treatments the doctors had first suggested. We wanted every fighting chance we could get. Driving back home, without our time in the chemo suite, we tried to make light of our worries by recalling a scene from *Seinfeld* when the "Soup Nazi" decides who he'll serve. "No soup for you," he'd yell at an annoying customer.

"No soup for you today," Peter and I both said aloud in the car on the way home.

As the radiation continued, the doses got stronger. By the end of the twenty-five sessions, Peter had had as much radiation as a body could take. But even so, he didn't experience the extreme fatigue so many others do. One day at the Juravinski he got on the elevator on the ground floor to go down one flight to the radiation suite. A young woman got on with him and fell asleep standing in the elevator between floors. Peter had to wake her up when the doors opened. For him, a rest in bed after we drove home seemed to be all he needed. The lack of any harsh side effects gave us the feeling — perhaps the illusion — that the treatments were working, that Peter wasn't that ill. For logical people like us, it was fanciful thinking, but sometimes that's what you need to get through the day.

Peter never liked obituaries about people who had "lost their battle with cancer" or "fought bravely against cancer." He didn't see the disease in military terms, never thought of himself as heroic. During his treatments, he preferred to say he was having "an argument with cancer," as if he could talk it down. With his skills of memory and his ability to organize his thoughts, thanks to a lawyer's training, he rarely lost an argument with anyone, including me. But I suppose he knew that cancer was the one final argument he could lose. We never talked about it, though. I understood him well enough to know that by not talking about death he was keeping it at bay. At least in his mind if not in his body. To keep on going, he had to believe he would recover.

I could never see cancer in debating terms. I saw cancer as a terrorist fighting a dirty war, with rogue cells attacking the good cells in Peter's body, determined to destroy them and kill him. Medical treatments, good nutrition, and rest were the only weapons in the arsenal of our defence. And optimism that Peter would win this argument/war.

For me, more and more, the Victory Garden I was envisioning became my weapon of that optimism. I had to stop reading the cancer literature and warnings, which did little but scare me once I knew what danger signs to watch for. I needed to read about Victory Gardens to find out how to grow an abundance of nutritious, beautiful food. And I wanted to find some characters from the past who would inspire me to not lose hope.

I found the first reference to Victory Gardens in readings about Great Britain and the First World War. My image of a country of rolling green lands and productive farms took a hit as I discovered that Great Britain was importing more than half of its food when it entered the war in 1914. A year later, when Kaiser Wilhelm II threatened to destroy all ships headed to British shores in retaliation for a British naval blockade of Germany, the spectre of food shortages and the fear of starvation became very real. Compensating for the lack of imported food became a matter of patriotism. A government campaign urged gardeners to grow their own vegetables and fruits to beat the U-boats.

Already, I knew the garden taking shape in my mind had only a thin connection to the wartime Victory Gardens, even if I thought of cancer in battle terms. I lived in a region where I could get a basket of peach "seconds" for a toonie and buy any fresh vegetables I wanted all year round. There were no shortages, no threats to my county's sovereignty. But the Victory Gardens of the war years were also about staring down uncertainty and finding nurture in the rhythm of digging, sowing, harvesting, and preserving, ideas I could hold on to like a lamppost in a storm.

I once stood in a perfectly manicured, colourful garden in Maryland on a June day, after the wedding of friends of ours. On one side of the backyard, beds were filled with beautiful flowers in full bloom. That was the wife's side of the house. The husband took Peter and me around to the other side of the house, away from the patio furniture and the cocktails, and showed us where his vegetable garden was laid out. "My wife doesn't want to have anything in the garden you can eat," he said. "I don't want to grow anything you can't."

That story came back to me when I read about the challenge the British government faced in the First World War to turn landowners' notion of a garden upside down. Just say the words *English garden* and you evoke an image of scented roses, colourful lilies, and blue delphiniums; of wide lawns and clipped hedges; and for some, a Jane Austen heroine with her flower-picking basket, oblivious to where the food on her table comes from. The flower garden had long been a symbol of English gentility, a sought-after sign of wealth and leisure, something that Maryland wife would have agreed with. And her husband and my father would greatly dispute.

Vegetables were rarely grown by the British middle or upper classes; instead, they came from the rough farms managed by lower-class workers in their drab clothes and muddy boots. Or they came packed on ships from distant lands along with exotic spices and fruit.

But that had to change if people wanted to eat. The government urged homeowners to replace their flower beds and even their lawns with vegetable gardens. It was nothing short of their duty. The government also converted land lying idle across the nation, so-called slacker land, into a million allotment or community gardens for those without property. Vegetables, not roses, would preserve the British way of life.

The message sunk in slowly. It's hard, it seems, to turn a rose cultivator into a turnip grower. By 1917, the British hadn't produced enough food for the last year of the war. They had to turn to the United States with a request for millions of bushels of wheat to keep their nation fed.

Before the Americans entered the war in 1917, President Woodrow Wilson sagely recognized the danger of food shortages in Great Britain and Europe. On the continent, young men had been pulled away from farms to join armies, and farmland lay in ruin from chemicals and shelling.

Wilson recognized that food was key not just to winning the war but to maintaining the peace that would inevitably come to

Europe. He saw that if food shortages persisted on the other side of the Atlantic, world chaos would ensue. I couldn't help admiring his foresight and his commitment to making sure that didn't happen. He urged the passing of the Lever Food and Fuel Control Act, created the United States Food Administration, and appointed a retired engineer, a future president, Herbert Hoover, to encourage Americans to conserve food so the country would be able to feed the hungry of Europe.

In this new role, Hoover called on Americans to cut back their diets. Eating less became popularly known as *Hooverizin'*. Hoover pushed recipes with just a few ingredients, including one for Victory Bread, made without flour. He reached into American kitchens with cookbooks, a regime of Meatless Tuesdays and Wheatless Wednesdays, and a list of rules: "Food. 1 — buy it with thought. 2 — cook it with care. 3 — serve just enough. 4 — save what will keep. 5 — eat what would spoil. 6 — home-grown is best."

I've never identified with American presidents, but I did find some inspiration in a timberman named Charles Lathrop Pack, who joined the campaign to find better ways to save food, although he, too, was entitled. He was one of America's wealthiest men, but he took on his assignment in those war years with such gusto, it was hard not to admire his creative energy. He was the man who ran with Hoover's rule number 6: "home-grown is best." Perhaps I admired him most of the cadre of men involved in food projects because he wanted to see Americans in their yards, growing vegetables.

To get Americans out in their gardens, he organized the National War Garden Commission and kick-started a vigorous campaign to promote vegetable gardens by distributing free gardening books and appealing to the press and community groups across the country. After the war, he wrote a book about the Victory Garden movement in America. "Before the people would spring to the hoe, as they instinctively sprang to the rifle," he wrote, "they had to be shown, and shown conclusively, that the bearing of one implement was as patriotic a duty as the carrying of the other. Only persistent publicity, only continual preachment, could convince the public of that."

The preaching came in the form of posters with cartoon-like vegetables as heroes and slogans like "The Seeds of Victory Insure the Fruits of Peace." In one poster, grunting vegetables climb over a wall accompanied by the words "War Gardens Over the Top." In another, carrots, potatoes, and tomatoes hold high an American flag and march behind a boy with a hoe slung over his shoulder. "War Gardens Victorious," screams the poster. I loved those feisty vegetables. I loved how they were fighting.

To remind civilians, or "soldiers of the soil" as Pack called them, why their gardens mattered, one poster showed the kaiser squished into a canning bottle, which stood between a bottle of tomatoes and a bottle of peas: "Can Vegetables, Fruit, And the Kaiser too."

But perhaps the most blatant appeal to patriotism was a poster of a tall woman resembling Lady Liberty. Dressed in a full-length gown made of the American flag, she sowed seeds in a wide field, her bare alabaster arms untouched by either sun or dirt. I had to laugh at the purity of the image. Whenever I garden, my hands, my face, and especially the knees of my jeans end up covered in dirt. And I love it. I already knew my Victory Garden would be a gloriously messy affair.

That image of the palest of women no doubt targeted the people Pack wanted in the garden: white Americans with farms or suburban houses of their own. While I identified more with the chubby, happy vegetables than with the elegant female gardener, I felt a moment of gratitude for my own privilege of having a big enough yard to grow food that would nurture both Peter and me.

Even though the American Victory Garden campaign started later, its propaganda campaign fired the public imagination and in the end proved more effective than the British one. Pack's campaign inspired songs with corny titles like "Keep the Home Soil Turning," as well as hackneyed poetry: "We've got to dig in our back yards for carrots, beans, and 'taters; we've got to dig both long and hard as garden cultivators. So take your trusty hoe and spade and start your spring-time sowing. Just dig and get a garden made and set the foodstuff growing." Cities around the country responded with War Garden Days and parades of marching students followed by floats filled with vegetables. And backyard gardens everywhere.

By 1918, according to Pack, Americans had dug up more than five million war gardens, on both private and public lands. After the war, Pack tried to keep gardeners digging to support the continued needs of Europe. "The War Garden of 1918," he wrote, "must become the Victory Garden of 1919." But without a war as incentive, without fear, many simply hung up their hoes.

The same thing happened in Great Britain. In the years between the great wars, the island became even more dependent on imports. On the eve of the Second World War, about 70 percent of its food came from elsewhere. Most of the onions Brits ate came from Europe, their fruit came from Australia and South Africa, wheat from North America, tomatoes from the Netherlands, and apples from France.

In retrospect, it was stupid to stop campaigns after the signing of the Treaty of Versailles that were making a difference in how people saw food. But that's human nature, it seems. We forget lessons when we don't need them, once we can live our lives with our old complacency. I understood. I longed for the days when I wouldn't have to visit cancer centres or read about survival statistics. When I could be blasé about the threat to the plans we had for our life together.

As I buoyed myself reading about how people fought an enemy with food, Peter distracted himself with dark mystery novels by the likes of Jo Nesbo and Ian Rankin and the darkest dramas he could find on Netflix. That was one of the differences between us. When things got dark, Peter liked to go darker. I needed light to stave off depression. So, as the treatments ended and we entered the period of waiting before Peter could have the scan that would reveal if surgery was possible, I kept reading about Victory Gardens, looking for the seeds of our own victory, looking for a role model.

The next chapter of the Victory Garden came in the Second World War. With another war and new threats of blockades, British bureaucrats in the Ministry of Agriculture dusted off the old campaigns, pumped them up, and came up with a catchy slogan: "Dig for Victory."

"All the potatoes, all the cabbages, and all the other vegetables we can produce may be needed," the minister said. "That is why I appeal to you, lovers of this great country of ours, to dig, to cultivate, to sow, and to plant."

In a series of Dig for Victory leaflets, the government gave advice on, well, how to dig, but also how to sow, handle pests, and choose the right vegetables for winter storage. The British would need parsnips, carrots, potatoes, kale, cabbage, and leeks to get them through the cold months of bombardments. The government added more allotment gardens for urban dwellers. And after German bombing raids scarred the country, creating extra slacker land, boys' clubs took up the job of clearing away rubble to grow more vegetables. One photograph from the war epitomizes that British carry-on sentiment; it shows a London couple cultivating their round lush garden planted in a bomb crater. I never found out who they were, but I wanted their determination.

In Canada, at the beginning of the war, the government actively discouraged amateur gardeners; it feared they would waste valuable resources like garden tools, fertilizers, and sprays needed in the military's war effort. But as more food was sought for Great Britain and troops abroad and the effects of rationing began to be felt at home, those amateur gardeners took to their gardens anyway, calling them Victory Gardens even if the government wouldn't. In 1942, a group in Victoria that called itself the Victory Garden Brigade petitioned the Minister of Agriculture to give his support to Victory Gardeners. By then, clothing stores were already offering summery fashions for the Victory Gardeners and Toronto's Eaton's department store was selling rakes, hoes, and plant food in its Garden Grove shop for Victory Garden needs. In June of 1942, the *Globe and Mail* reported that the most popular book in Toronto libraries was called *25 Vegetables and How to Grow Them.* "This rather startling piece of information," the article continued somewhat breathlessly, "was furnished by Miss Anne Wright, head of the circulation department of the Toronto Public Libraries. It seems Toronto citizens like the Victory Garden idea and are storming the libraries to learn how to make drills and keep the cut-worms away from tomatoes, and the cabbage-butterflies off the cabbages."

By the growing season of 1943, the government gave in and officially supported Victory Gardens in backyards and on public lands. The Health League of Canada started a Vegetables for Victory campaign focusing on the nutritional value of vegetables. While its slogan — "Help Canada and have fun, too!" — was far less dramatic than the British slogan, by 1943 more than two hundred thousand Victory Gardens had sprouted in Canada, up about 25 percent from the beginning of the war.

It took the attack on Pearl Harbor on December 7, 1941, to get Americans not only into the war but back into their gardens. Twelve days after the attack, the government hurriedly brought back campaigns and started new institutes to educate the public on how food would bring victory. "Food fights for freedom," President Franklin Roosevelt said. "For food — American food — can be the deadliest weapon of all. It may save thousands of American lives. The course and length of the war may depend on how successfully we produce it — how willingly and widely we share it — how carefully we save it, how wisely we use it." First Lady Eleanor Roosevelt did her part by having the White House lawn dug up for a Victory Garden. And once again vegetables appeared on posters as heroes, this time bombing a swastika. "*You* can make this kind of ammunition," one poster exhorted.

Annual conferences with representatives from all levels of government outlined the goals for each growing season: Let's increase the twenty million Victory Gardens of 1943 to twenty-two million. Let's have twenty-six million home preservers. Let's manufacture sixty million pressure cookers. The main message: Victory Gardeners *can* and *must* do a still better job.

Conference organizers held sessions on canning beets, on the shortages of rubber hoses and seeds. They discussed the best pesticides to use to surmount shortages caused by the war. "The supplies of lead arsenate, nicotine sulphate, the newer cryolite seem to be adequate," said one report. They encouraged gardeners to get the most out of the limited supply of rotenone insecticides — insecticides that kill leaf-eating caterpillars and, incidentally, fish — by getting out earlier in the season with dusters and sprays, "while the bugs are fewer and more susceptible."

I got a lot of practical ideas about my Victory Garden by reading reports from the conferences. I learned not to grow too many different types of vegetables in the garden so I wouldn't get overwhelmed with the knowledge required to care for each kind. I learned to divide the garden between leafy vegetables that could be eaten in the spring and summer and root vegetables, tomatoes, and squash that could be preserved or stored for winter. I learned that successive sowings of seeds stretched the abundance of the garden, lengthened the season, and controlled waste. And I read it was wise to leave corn and potatoes to the farmers who had the space. But I already knew that.

I also decided, as I read conference reports, what I would do differently. Wartime Victory Gardens were intended to produce the heaviest crops possible. The only way to achieve that was through pesticides. Lots of them. I already knew that part of my victory would be in creating an organic garden that didn't tax our health or the environment, even if I didn't get enough vegetables for an entire year.

I still can picture my father in his sweaty T-shirt and cap driving the tractor up and down the rows of cherry and peach trees on our farm, pulling the sprayer behind him. I remember the sprayer as a big tank that spewed out chemicals I could smell from the back porch of our house. I remember one of the chemicals my father used was Captan, later identified as carcinogenic. I don't remember my father wearing any special gear or mask; I'm sure it never occurred to him. And although he never developed cancer, he did have weak lungs and a propensity for pneumonia throughout his later life. In his eighties, his lungs were so scarred that during his last bout of pneumonia, he could no longer breathe. Just as I'll never know if Captan led to my father's lung ailments, I'll never know what role environmental toxins played in giving Peter cancer. But my Victory Garden would be pesticide-free, a small contribution to clean air.

After 1945, the conferences ended; campaigns disappeared. Surprise, surprise. The war was over. The term *Victory Garden* largely disappeared from government material, resurfacing occasionally in the media in times of political and economic uncertainty. As author Cecilia Gowdy-Wygant points out in her book *Cultivating Victory*, postwar gardens were more about personal survival than they were about patriotism and helping others, more about protecting an individual's world than creating community. "Many modern adaptations shun such ideas as aspects of a bygone era and instead move toward self-preservation."

Gowdy-Wygant writes that self-preservation gardens popped up after crises, such as the hoarding period leading up to Y2K and during the wars that came after 9/11, when the world order made little sense. But I found my favourite survivalist garden movement online. The Zombie Victory Garden website offered insight into growing vegetables to prepare for the zombie apocalypse. Their motto: "The Zombies Are Coming! Quick! Plant Something!"

And then in 2009, a second Victory Garden appeared on the White House lawn. This one had nothing to do with a shortage of food, but rather with an overabundance of the wrong kind of food. First Lady Michelle Obama introduced her organic garden to educate children about the dangers of obesity and diabetes. Her battle was against processed food laden with sugar, salt, and fat; her rallying cry was "Let's hear it for vegetables!" She could have used Charles Lathrop Pack in her campaign. Kids would have loved his kick-ass vegetables.

The spirit of the Victory Garden survives in urban community gardens that offer fresh produce to locals who might not otherwise have access to it. And it lives on in the marketing of developers who have caught on to consumer interest in sustainability. Those developers are creating housing communities across North America, known as agrihoods, communities not built around golf courses, wide-open green spaces, or water features, but around gardens and orchards that can supply the needs of those who live in the neighbourhoods.

After I read all I could about wartime Victory Gardens and their legacy, I had no illusion mine would influence anyone's eating habits, keep me safe in an apocalypse of any kind, or effect positive change in the world. But maybe, secretly, I hoped that if I worked hard to create something good, something good would come to us in the form of a cure for Peter's cancer. But that secret, that twisted logic of magical thinking, was buried deeper in my mind than the garlic cloves in my garden.

Throughout my reading, I discovered no single person who could become my gardening inspiration. Not even Charles Lathrop Pack, the man on a mission; I just couldn't imagine such a rich man getting his own hands dirty. But as a loner, I've always found it hard to find mentors. And I knew I'd have to go it alone in my garden without a great figure from history watching over my shoulder. As I filed away my notes and articles on the war-time Victory Gardens, I realized that it didn't matter. I didn't need some unknown character as my inspiration. I had memories of a grandmother — my mother's mother — who grew vegetables in a kitchen garden inside a white picket fence. And I had my father. Everyday people, my ancestors, who wanted to take control of their own food and feed those they loved. They would be my silent models as I began to turn the soil in my garden and carry out my own fight for victory.

Chapter Four

WHAT WAS I THINKING?

By late January, I wondered. I didn't feel I'd ever be organized and focused enough to carry through with my plans for a Victory Garden. We still had no word on whether the radiation and chemotherapy treatments had done their job and Peter could have surgery. No appointment for that crucial CT scan with its thumbs-up or thumbs-down. And here I was plotting a Victory Garden.

Who was I kidding?

It would be too self-deprecating for me to suggest I haven't accomplished things in my life, completed difficult projects, even been successful now and again. And over my lifetime I'd developed the muscle to get up and get on after failure. But the word *victory* seemed too strong, and, in winter, a Victory Garden too grand an ambition. The possibility that I could design and source the garden and then nurture all those plants overwhelmed me when I looked out my office window at the cold, barren vegetable patch. Especially with the gnawing fear in my belly about the odds of victory over cancer, especially when, in the depths of winter, all I really wanted to do was read cozy mystery novels, rewatch favourite series on DVD, and stay in bed as late into the morning as I could.

There's a book I love about writing, Anne Lamott's *Bird by Bird*. In it, her father calms his panicked son who has left a school project on birds until the last moment. "Bird by bird," he tells him. That story taught me that while I needed to keep the whole problem, the whole project in mind, I'd have to approach it bird by bird, word by word, step by step. So I started with the smallest piece: the seeds. At first I thought that was clever, so when I sat down at my computer, instead of looking at cancer statistics, I searched online catalogues for inspiration and ideas about the plants and varieties I'd want. And I did feel that exhilaration of taking a first step.

One morning I found a seed company online that was offering free shipping for orders placed by February first. It seemed like a sign to get busy. I quickly filled a virtual shopping cart with seeds to beat the deadline, even though, somewhere in the back of my mind, I knew buying seeds was not the right "bird" to start with.

By the time I had nineteen dollars worth of seeds in the cart — some old standbys, some untried — I was ready to check out. It was then I noticed that the free shipping was only offered for shipments of one hundred dollars or more. I closed the site, relieved that I hadn't got ahead of myself. I ended my morning by bookmarking other promising seed catalogues so I wouldn't feel I'd wasted my time. And, when companies had them, I ordered print catalogues like the ones my father had read again and again, with pictures I could circle and margins I could write lists in so I could ponder my choices, not rush into them.

When the first catalogue arrived, I was disappointed. Although Heritage Harvest Seed, based in Manitoba, called their small booklet an "illustrated catalogue," its pages held only a scattering of black-and-white historic-looking drawings, perhaps designed to assure buyers the seeds sold were as pure as some imagined past. But I'm a visual person — a photographer, a former documentary producer. I wanted full-colour photos of shiny red tomatoes, deep-green chard, and cucumbers shot so close I could see the prickles on them. I told myself I'd wait for other catalogues, the ones from the big seed houses. I was getting used to waiting anyway. Most of the days of late January were spent that way, wondering whether the stray cancer cells in Peter's lymph system, the ones that made his cancer Stage 3, had been bombarded out of his body as the tumour was zapped.

The glossy catalogues were slow in coming, so I found myself on the last Saturday in January sitting with the sun streaming in through the windows of the great room, a cooling cup of coffee at my side, immersed in the Heritage Harvest Seed catalogue and its seventy-four pages of "UNTREATED NATURAL SEEDS." Even though I was far from finalizing my seed selection, the booklet got me thinking about how many plants I would start from seed and how many I'd buy as seedlings from a nursery. Vegetables like radishes, chard, carrots, and lettuces grow easily from seed, but others, like onions, tomatoes, and squash, would grow faster from seedlings, and without a greenhouse, I didn't want to take on the task of germinating all my seeds indoors, timing their growth for the right moment for transplanting into the earth.

I marvelled at the number of seeds listed by Heritage Harvest Seed that I'd never heard of. "Very rare." "Seed exclusive." "EXTREMELY RARE." Some seeds seemed worth buying for the seller's narrative alone. Take this pole bean, Tung's bean:

Preserved by the Kerr family of Long Beach, BC since the early 1900's. In 1906 James D. Kerr immigrated from England and settled at Long Beach on Kootenay Lake. He hired a Chinese laborer, by the name of Tung to help him on his new 50 acre property. Mr. Tung was in charge of the vegetable garden and planted these beans that he had brought from China. After 25 years Mr. Tung returned to his homeland and the beans were preserved by the Kerr family.

My God, I thought, *there's a global novel in that seed.*

How did the Kerrs treat Mr. Tung, I wondered. Why did he leave China and then go back after a quarter of a century? If I grew the beans, would I be able to taste what Mr. Tung had tasted? I felt especially sad for Mr. Tung's displacement. Living with someone with cancer, seeing how many people struggled in and out of the Juravinski Cancer Centre every day, often left me weepy.

As tempting as the narrative for Tung's beans was, I'd already decided on Kentucky Wonder for my pole beans because of my own narrative. They were my father's beans, the ones he and my mother blanched and chilled for the freezer. And I'd grown them for years from seeds I overwintered in the basement. An envelope was waiting in the dark cold room for the spring.

The other choices in the catalogue were simply overwhelming: 189 types of tomatoes and 26 types of lettuce, including one called Drunken Woman, described as an "Italian leaf lettuce with reddish edges." It was the first seed I circled. I had to have it if only to point it out to visitors while we sipped red wine in the yard.

I stopped in the middle of counting the number of squash seeds available and wondered how my father had made his choices. Did he ever just pick a seed for its name or by its description alone? I knew he liked to experiment; he tried planting peanuts in Ontario before others did, grew gourds before they started to appear in market shops each fall. He sent me back to university with oddly shaped green and orange bumpy gourds that became a source of wonderment and amusement to the residents on my dormitory floor. After my father, a self-taught musician who played multiple instruments, read how Africans make music with gourds, he dried his own so that when we shook them the seeds knocked against the taut skin. To my embarrassment, he even cut an oversized dry gourd shaped like a banjo in half, painted it gold, and stuck some cotton batting and a plastic Santa Claus in it. It hung by a red ribbon on our dining room wall as a Christmas decoration for years.

When I was in my twenties, married, and living in a basement apartment with my first, still-student husband, I appealed to my father's sense of experimentation. I'd bought into the seventies' back-to-the-land movement. Big time. Even though I had no land. In an old-style food store in Guelph with wide and worn pine floorboards, my husband and I ground our own peanut butter. We baked with honey, soaked beans and legumes. We gave up sugar after reading the fear-raising book *Sugar Blues* and trusted in the power of herbs after reading the classic *Back to Eden*.

I don't remember seeing tofu in the grocery stores back then, but I came to believe we had to have soya beans in our diet. So I asked my father to plant some for me, and he did. That fall he showed up on our doorstep with several bushel baskets full of long drying pods. I shelled them and put the small white beans in big glass jars. Where they sat and sat. I tried making soups with them, tried disguising them as Boston brown beans. But as they slowly cooked, they filled the apartment with a loathsome odour. It didn't matter how I spiced them or sauced them; they always came out tasting like gasoline. I pushed the jars to the back of the cupboard where they stayed out of mind until our next move, when I could feel good about clearing out my shelves.

But no matter how willing my father was to try new plants, he always made sure he made enough room for his standbys in his garden between the cherry trees. And in that, there seemed to be a good lesson for me: the garden for the joy of play and experimentation as well as the serious business of feeding a family. After that realization, I knew I'd have rows of standard beets and carrots embracing the Drunken Woman.

Before I could figure out my mix of reliable and chancy varieties, I knew what I had to do as my first bird, my first step: measure my two vegetable beds and see how they compared to the old Victory Garden map I'd found. Only then could I begin drawing my own map with the number of rows I could have and see what vegetables I could reasonably include. I knew I had to do that, but I didn't do it. For days, "measure the garden" was on my to-do list stuck to my computer monitor and was the one thing left undone when I turned off my desk lamp at night. The ground was bare; I could see the space I had to measure from the back windows of the house, but still I didn't do it. The days were a bit colder the last week in January but not *that* cold. Call it inertia, fear of failure, whatever. I just couldn't take that necessary step.

At least, by that stage in my life, I'd come to recognize that January is my worst month, a month when I can't really accomplish anything. In the heart of winter, my doubts and my sense of failure are always strongest. *How many jobs have I walked away from? How many friendships have I screwed up? How many opportunities have I wasted? WILL I EVER GET ANYTHING RIGHT?*

In January, there is a stillness that calls for introspection. The bare limbs of the trees speak of basics, of the essence of things. When I drive in my new home territory of Niagara in winter, the rows of stark grapevines and fruit trees, without the clothing of leaves, reveal their primary shapes, their skeletons, and demand that I look beneath the layers of my daily activities, my plans, my wishes, to my deepest core. And that January, when the hold was tenuous on all we had, as we waited for Peter to heal enough for his CT scan, my bones felt completely exposed. Peter always empathized with my winter depression. That and his fear of walking on ice with his unsteady gait were why we had designed our new lives to include a month away each winter.

Bird by bird, I told myself.

Before the month of January ended, I would measure the space for the Victory Garden. In February, I would plot my map and decide what I'd grow in my beds. And then spring would not be far off once the days started getting longer. And I'd get started. I would follow the inspiration of my father, who used the rhythm of the garden season, the miracle of seeds, the abundance of crops to carry him forward.

Chapter Five

BY THE LAST DAY OF JANUARY that year, I still had not measured my two vegetable beds, although I had no excuse. I certainly had the free time, and the weather was with me. The month ended with temperatures usually granted to us in northern climes early in the spring. The sun, with surprising heat to it, urged me to get out in the yard and get the job done.

I knew my two patches would not come close to the twenty-five-by-fifty-foot garden carefully plotted on the Second World War Victory Garden map I'd chosen as my example. That would be 1,250 square feet, the size of a bungalow. Bigger than most city apartments.

My problem: how to get an accurate measurement with two beds that were not even shapes. Modern surveyors can precisely measure the area of any space by using skills in geometry, engineering, and physics and with tools like infrared refractors and something called a robotic total station. The RTS, I learned, is a modern piece of surveying equipment that allows one surveyor to measure with remote controls — modern, I suppose, in its use of robotics and in eliminating jobs.

I possessed none of these things, neither the skills nor the equipment. I'd have to rely on the time-tested method of measuring a farmer's irregular field. It involves dividing the field into triangles or other measurable shapes, figuring out the area of each shape, and then adding them all together. Math skills have never been my strong suit but I thought I could manage this puzzle.

Wearing a pair of old running shoes that squished in the muddy earth and armed with a measuring tape, paper, and pencil, I set out, feeling like I was finally beginning something. Like I was shaking off the month's inaction. Being on hold, not knowing what would come next in Peter's care had raised our anxiety to heights we hadn't felt since we first received the diagnosis. When we had been driving back and forth to Hamilton for treatments, we felt, at least, a sense we were doing something to beat back the cancer. This waiting left me feeling languid and helpless. Like I was touching a wire with a low current that ran continuously through me. It was no wonder I kept hearing, in my head, the Leonard Cohen song "Bird on the Wire."

But by the last day of January, we felt we were at the edge of something happening. In early February, we would start to get some answers again. And I knew that once I had my measurements, I could get on with all the other steps. Peter and I were both organizers, planners, by inclination and profession; we both desperately needed a schedule and an outcome.

That morning, cloaked in just a light spring jacket, I measured the bigger plot first, the one I'd used the previous summer. It was basically a rectangle with two pear trees I'd planted in corners. Eventually, those trees would grow, provide shade, and decrease the size of the vegetable garden, but not that year, not the year of my Victory Garden. I stood in the yard without a sound around me except the caw of a crow in a tree nearby that seemed perturbed a human would enter its space in winter. I tsked at it while

I measured the garden in squares and triangles. I wrote the numbers on my paper, multiplied, and came up with a measurement of basically twenty-two feet by twenty feet. Only 440 square feet.

The other, smaller bed was trickier to measure. It was shaped like a boat, with curving lines and narrow ends. I had dug out a mass of sedum that had filled the bed, given the bed some compost and manure, and used one end of it for my garlic in the fall. In that end stood our garden's most magnificent tree, a columnar flowering dogwood that had been completely covered in blossoms from May to July the previous year. In the centre of the bed, I'd planted a garden-size Stella cherry and at the far end a Montmorency sour cherry. They, too, would command much of the sun within a few years. If I still wanted a Victory Garden then, I'd have to come up with another vegetable bed. But the ifs were elusive and daunting. *If* I was still gardening. *If* we were still in this house. *IF.* I tried not to think about them. Filed the doubts away.

For the smaller bed, I worked with the average width of 5 feet and the length of 22 feet to come up with a size of approximately 110 square feet for my allium — I would plant red onions and leeks in among the garlic already in the ground — and my *Cucurbita* varieties (summer and winter squash), which I would plant at the other end.

All in all, I had 550 square feet for vegetables, less than half of my model map. To put it in metric terms, I had 51 square metres as opposed to the 116 square metres of the Victory Garden I'd found on the internet. But that was okay. I had a separate bed for herbs, a small patch with rhubarb, and another for berry canes. As well, I'd planted spreading strawberries to run through a flower bed and three native pawpaw trees, which would bear their papaya-like fruit in a few years. We were not a family of five trying to get through a year of war scarcity. We were two people and would have more than enough from our beds, with plenty to spare for Jane and neighbours. And if the zombie apocalypse did come, I could churn up more lawn another year.

With the measuring finished, the next step was filling in my maps with rows so I would finally see how many varieties of vegetables I could plant and could decide what seeds to order. But before I got around to that we got caught up again in Peter's treatment. Peter received word his CT scan would happen on February fifth and the follow-up appointment with the surgeon on February sixteenth. Surgery, if it happened, could be as far away as a month after that.

About that time, two glossy catalogues appeared in my mailbox. I decided to set them aside, thinking they'd be a good way to wile away the time in February, with its second round of waiting. But before I did, I flipped through the pages and admired the bright greens, oranges, and reds that screamed out flavour and nutrients, that made me feel real excitement about the potential of those beds I'd measured.

It also didn't escape me during that time that my obsession with a project involving healthy vegetables was linked to my worries about Peter and food. With his swallowing problems, he found it a relentless chore to take in enough nourishment.

Getting food into patients is a major concern for any medical staff treating esophageal cancer. When we had finally landed at the Juravinski Cancer Centre in Hamilton in November, one of the first questions the brilliant radiologist Dr. S asked Peter was "Are you eating?" Dr. S is one of the leading specialists in a treatment called brachytherapy; the Juravinski was the only cancer centre in Canada then where patients could receive it. While the treatment can't kill the cancer, it can reduce the tumour's size enough so that food can make it to the stomach more easily, meaning patients can eat to keep up strength and endure their treatments.

Even before the oncology team prescribed the regime of radiation blasts and supporting chemo sessions, Dr. S gave Peter three brachytherapy sessions. Essentially, in brachytherapy, a pellet of radioactive material is sent down the esophagus in a tube to sit directly by the tumour, where it is left for a few minutes.

While waiting with Peter as he was prepped each time for the procedure, I could hear Dr. S through the curtains surrounding Peter's bed scolding patients who weren't eating. One man, whom I later saw was rail thin, told Dr. S that, although he hadn't eaten anything that day, he had drunk four bottles of Ensure. We had just begun buying the nutritional supplement to get enough calories into Peter, but he was loath to rely on it. We heard other patients complain that food just didn't taste good anymore so they'd stopped eating. Dr. S told patients that the cancer cells were suppressing their appetite. *Those nasty buggers*, I thought. Dr. S warned patients lying in beds beyond the curtains that if they didn't keep eating, he'd have to insert a feeding tube to get the nutrition and calories they needed into their bodies. Those were fighting words to Peter; he said he'd do anything to avoid a feeding tube, and he was a stubborn enough man to stick to his word. He continued eating when it was the last thing he wanted to do.

Before the radiation started in earnest, Dr. S warned Peter that he would have to maintain his body weight even though his swallowing would become worse before it got better. Everyone on the team at the Juravinski Centre advised Peter to eat lots of calories, protein, and fat. And they didn't want him to build up his immune system when he was going through treatments that were purposely intended to suppress it while killing the cancerous cells.

When the dietitian on the team recommended that Peter not bother with vegetables during this stage of his treatment, I was horrified. I grew up believing everyone needs four servings of vegetables a day, because that's what my mother put in front of me most evenings. I could just as easily chomp on radishes and celery than cheese. Peter never shared my fondness for raw vegetables or for the array of vegetables I love, so that request didn't bother him as much as it did me.

But he was alarmed when the dietitian wrote down the number of calories and the amount of protein he would need to include in his diet to deal with the added stress on his body the treatments would cause: 2,500 to 3,000 calories a day, more than the recommended amount for a man his age. And 125 to 300 grams of protein a day, for a man who didn't eat much meat. All at a time when he had no appetite.

In the days leading up to his first radiation treatment, Peter had what they call a planning CT. During the procedure, a young man tattooed permanent points onto Peter's body where the radiation needed to enter to reach the cancer cells. The technician warned us that if Peter lost 10 percent of his body mass, the target points would no longer match up to the right areas. I pictured a bull's eye and misaimed arrows.

That meant Peter had to force himself to eat, like a duck making foie gras — although he took the role of both duck and enforcer. We had to come up with calorie-rich foods that could go down easily: blended legume and vegetable soups, macaroni and cheese, ice cream, meat lasagna, and smoothies. For some reason Peter could eat poached eggs but not scrambled. Each morning I made a smoothie of whey powder, Greek yogurt, fruit, and, with the permission of the dietitian, powdered greens.

During the treatments, Peter's swallowing did become worse. Not only was the shrinking tumour still in his esophagus blocking the passage of food, the esophagus itself became raw and more painful after each radiation session. We never ate out and Peter wouldn't eat in front of anyone but me and Jane because each bite came with a potential coughing jag that could last twenty minutes, making him feel he would regurgitate everything he ate. He never did and, through sheer willpower, he managed to keep his weight steady.

Because of his difficulties with eating and his need to keep away from anyone ill, we begged off all Christmas parties and family dinners. I baked the lasagna Jane, Peter, and I liked to eat for Christmas Eve and we made a relatively traditional Christmas dinner. For the few times we'd had Christmas in our own home in the past, Peter had loved to roast the turkey, prepare a big dish of stuffing, and mash his smooth potatoes. He always prepared his potatoes even when we visited someone in my family for Christmas dinner; everyone loved his mashed potatoes.

Jane and I ate heartily at both meals that year, but Peter took small servings of the dishes and took his time with each bite. He couldn't taste the flavours the way he had in the past. There was no smacking of his lips, no second helpings. For him, though, the Christmastime meals were made special by the doctor's permission to have a glass of white wine with each one.

Through it all, I ate and ate. Oh, there were vegetables and healthy foods. But there were also second and third helpings I didn't need but took anyway as I watched in distress as Peter struggled with each forkful of food. If it had been summer, I would have stood in the garden eating raw beans and tomatoes, pulling up carrots and radishes, picking at the kale and lettuce. But it was winter and I ate too much pasta, potatoes, and chocolate.

After the treatments, the doctors had told us we'd have to wait weeks for the CT scan and the surgery, until some of the rawness and swelling in the esophagus healed. But sometimes I think doctors give explanations that suit their schedule. On the fourth of February, Peter received a call from the surgeon's office at St. Joseph's Hospital in Hamilton moving the CT scan up to that day. We'd also been told it would take a few days to process the information from the scan into a report. But suddenly those days were apparently unnecessary. Within an hour, Peter received a second call advising him to see the surgeon, Dr. F, right after the CT. Dr. F could read the CT scan himself.

With the scan done, we sat in the clinic's waiting room to see the doctor, neither of us voicing our fears or hopes. I closed my iPad Mah-Jong game that had got me through so much waiting and pulled out the two glossy seed catalogues I'd set aside. We talked quietly about the garden we'd sit in that summer. We'd limit the basil varieties in the herb bed to Thai and Genovese; neither of us had found last year's African or purple basil particularly tasty. I'd try tomatoes in pots, as well as in the garden, so we could easily grab them and enjoy their colour while we dined on the deck. We flipped pages and ignored other patients who rose to meet their doctors. We both knew we were distracting ourselves — but it was calming nonetheless. The vegetables were nurturing us even before the seeds were ordered and germinated.

After the waiting, everything moved as quickly as lettuce bolting in a sudden heat wave. Dr. F would do the surgery in ten days, not in a month's time. The CT showed the cancer had not spread, it was no longer in the lymph system, and radiation had reduced the tumour enough that it could be cut out. I raised the issue of the time needed for healing, but Dr. F said the date of surgery was within the protocol.

We left dazed but relieved. We had much to do before the surgery. Food remained the top priority. Peter had to maintain his weight and muscle mass so he'd be able to recover from what Dr. F called "routine but complicated surgery." Peter would lose the cancerous section of the esophagus and the remaining portion down to the stomach. Dr. F would then pull up the stomach to meet what was left of the esophagus. In the hospital, Peter would not be able to take anything orally, even chips of ice, for seven days after surgery to keep the internal stitches dry enough to heal. I suppose the team had told us this at our first meeting, but we'd shelved our worries then. Now, we realized how drastically the surgery would change Peter's life. Forever after, he would have to eat differently, never taking too much food at one time into a stomach that would be reduced in size by more than half. Suddenly, my Victory Garden seemed big enough.

Chapter Six

IN THE WEEK LEADING UP TO Peter's surgery, I tried to keep the garden alive in my mind, keep hope bouncing through my body. I skimmed through the catalogues, compared varieties, and circled seeds.

Although I've long been aware of the persuasive powers of good advertising and its clever copy, I wasn't immune to it. A zucchini in the Ontario Seed Company catalogue with the boring name of Dark Green was described as bearing "enough dark fruits to feed the nation." I circled it and underlined that key phrase. The zucchini seedlings I'd planted the previous year had overwhelmed us with produce. We'd eaten the small zucchini in stir-fries or grated and sautéed with olive oil and garlic, the larger ones in stews and baked breads, and the flowers fried in batter. But I still hadn't avoided waste. Some overgrown zucchinis rotted on the vine until blight brought a premature end to the plants' productivity. We vowed to use all the zucchini produced in the coming summer; the zucchini breads we'd stuck in the freezer had proven easy to bring out for overnight guests, and we could bake more.

Often, it was other, less clever phrases in the catalogue like "a good keeper," "quick maturity," or "frost tolerance" that caught my attention and influenced my choices.

Long before I took pen to paper, I'd formed in my mind a preliminary list of the vegetables I'd choose or reject. It went like this: Asparagus — No. Although I love their grassy flavour, I knew I didn't have space for enough plants to get a worthwhile crop. Besides, my father's failure with them scared me off. In our orchard, between rows of trees, he had created a second vegetable bed just for asparagus. Even though he'd have to wait years for tops worth eating, he tried planting them twice. Unfortunately, both times, when he rushed out to get at his cultivating the following spring, he forgot about his new beds and churned them up. After the second time, he never tried asparagus again.

Beans — Yes. I'd stick to my Kentucky Wonder bean seeds and I'd try a new bush bean, either something called Blue Lake, a customer favourite in the Stokes catalogue, or Ontario Seed Company's Jade II, described as having "traditional bean flavour" and "excellent disease resistance to common virus!"

Beets — Yes. Yes. Yes. Each time I bite into a beet I feel like my blood is getting richer. And I'm not wrong. Packed inside each beet, along with vitamin C, folate, and potassium, is the nutrient betaine, which supports the cardiovascular system. I love the earthy taste of beets cold or hot, boiled or roasted, in soups, in salads, or alone sliced on a plate with a drizzling of butter. Peter didn't like them much, although he'd eat clear borscht. So I'd be growing them mostly for myself and for the greens, which have a tangy taste that can stand alone or hold up in a stir-fry or pasta sauce.

I haven't always liked beet greens. As a child I was a picky eater and decided I didn't like beet greens even though I had never tasted them. My mother would take the leaves my father brought from his garden, boil them, and make them shine with butter, but they never tempted me. That changed, and now each time I eat beet greens they come with a side of memory.

My social skills, such as they are, came later in life. In public school, I never could figure out how to go about winning the friendship of another child or how far I should go to appease a bully. I tried to be a pleaser, and when that didn't work, I would simply retreat to my quiet spot alone.

One advantage I had with classmates was the rambling Victorian house we lived in. While I envied their neat suburban homes, they loved to explore my house, run up its curved staircase, or play on its upper veranda. And I liked to serve my house up to them. On the ground floor there was a dining room large enough to hold a table that could easily seat twelve, a long mahogany sideboard, and a tea tray with my mother's silver tea set. Looking back, I realize it was a grand room, but it was an ordinary one to me since our family ate there every Sunday. But it wasn't ordinary to the subdivision kids. To all of us, though, the most magnificent object in the room was the crystal chandelier that hung over the table.

When my parents took on the house after I was born, my father painstakingly restored each room. For years, the house had sat empty, except for two times when my grandfather had lent it to the town. During the Second World War, it served as quarters for farmerettes, as they were called in North America. They were single women who came from the cities to work on farms after the men left for war. Perhaps because of their diminutive name, I grew up thinking the farmerettes who'd lived in our house were all fun-loving teenage girls like Debbie Reynolds or Sandra Dee from the Tammy movies I'd watch on TV. And perhaps because I lived on a fruit farm, I always imagined those girls hanging cherries over their ears or dropping a cherry down the front of their blouses and when it didn't fall through, saying, like Tammy, "I'm a woman, fully growed." It was only later, when I read a little history, that I discovered that the British Women's Land Army, a very earnest organization, started in England and, during both world wars, sent thousands of land girls, single women of all ages, out in breeches and floppy hats to do heavy farm work, including ploughing. As a way of increasing food production, the program complemented the Victory Garden movement in both Great Britain and North America.

After the war, a fire destroyed the old hospital in town and our house become the local hospital for a time. My mother always told me my bedroom had been the nursery, although someone (maybe a brother) made me think it was where people were left to die.

As part of his renovation, my father had stripped the mahogany stair rail of its hospital green and wallpapered bedrooms and the hallway. And he'd hung that chandelier — the one my friends so admired — with great care. The chandelier had been a belated wedding gift my parents gave each other when their finances improved after the war. It was the most expensive and valued item in their home. To keep it from crashing onto the table, my father had taken up the pine boards in the bedroom above the dining room and bolted the chandelier to the floor joists. That chandelier wasn't going anywhere.

One day I was playing in the house with a couple of girls. My father was out in the orchard; my mother was sorting fruit in the barn. One of the girls — probably bossy Ruthy — said it would be fun to get up on one end of the dining-room table, grab the chandelier, and swing to the other end of the table. It was a popular idea, so I went along with it. And the girls seemed to have fun, although I can't really recall any swings I took. I've probably blocked them from my mind because my next memory is of my father coming into the room and yelling. The electrical cord of the chandelier had stretched and the chandelier now hung inches from the table. He yelled some more and said many things, but it was these words I can't forget: "I will never speak to you."

My father never struck me, but that day I wished he had. He was my garden pal. I rode with him to buy seeds and plants for his vegetable garden in the spring. I weeded and harvested with him in the summer. Even though he didn't talk much while we gardened, the idea he would never speak to me again stung.

Inexorably tied to the memory of his words was my first taste of beet greens. I sat beside him at the kitchen table that evening. My three older siblings had heard the story by then and were trying not to look too smug over the fact that for once it was the baby in trouble and not them. Dinner that night was the usual summer fare: some kind of cold meat, a turkey platter filled with sliced tomatoes from the garden, potatoes, green beans, and a dish of beet greens. To my father's surprise, I asked for beet greens. And I knew I had to eat them. I could feel him watching me as I took a forkful of the slimy greens and brought it to my mouth. I chewed them and swallowed. Their slight tartness seemed right for the occasion. I ate all my beet greens that evening and by the end discovered I loved them. I didn't say as much, but I knew that with each bite I was worming my way back into my father's heart. I've been a committed beet-green eater ever since.

Broccoli — Yes. I'd wanted to plant some in late summer the previous year for a fall crop but by then I couldn't find either seeds or plants. Now that I was committed to the idea of successive seed sowing, I wouldn't make that mistake again.

Cabbage — Yes. My inspirational Victory Garden map displayed both early and late cabbage. But I would make an adjustment to that. During the summer, there are so many other vegetables I prefer. I'd choose a variety — the name Multikeeper caught my eye — that I could store for the winter, when other fresh-vegetable choices disappeared. In the winter, I like to make a type of cabbage salad I'd discovered through my Russian friend. She grates the cabbage, salts it, and leaves it in a bowl with a weight on it for hours. Then she rinses the salt off the wilted cabbage, grates some carrots in with it, and dresses it with lemon juice and olive oil. I make a big batch of it and eat it for days in a row.

On and on my mental list grew. Carrots — Yes. Potatoes — No. Corn — No. I'd get both of those from local farmers. Cucumbers — Yes, but not the watery American kind, the Armenian heritage variety I'd spotted in my first catalogue. Eggplant — No, no, no. It's the one vegetable I despise. Kale — Definitely. My daughter, Jane, had gone through phases as a vegetarian, a vegan, and a juicer. Kale had been an element of all her diets. Lettuce — Yes, with attention to varieties that could cope with some heat so they wouldn't bolt and grow bitter at the first sign of real summer weather. Leeks — Yes, for Peter's favourite leek and potato soup, but only from sets. Onions — Yes, the red kind. Peppers — Yes, the red kind. Peas, radishes, and chard — All in. And, of course, zucchini to eat raw and cooked and baked in breads.

I spent the most time mulling over the last two vegetables: winter squash and tomatoes. Oh, I'd have them, but selecting the varieties would be difficult among all the choices every catalogue displayed.

Winter squash is one of the last foods that grows in the season and the best vegetable to keep; it stores well in cellars for months and fills the stomach cheaply with a wallop of vitamins. Squash is a food from here, the third vegetable in the Three Sisters trinity, with maize and beans, which has fed dwellers on the American continent for thousands of years. The genus *Cucurbita* demands time to reach its full, ripe size and space to spread its long vines.

In his garden, my father experimented with every kind of winter squash available to him: acorn; warty, thick-skinned Hubbard; bulbous butternuts; and orange pumpkins. My mother cooked them all. After my parents bought a deep freeze, they worked together in the kitchen filling tubs with baked squash for freezing. I came to dread Sunday dinners and the scoop of Hubbard squash that my mother plopped on my plate beside three other vegetables before passing the plate to my father for a slice of roasted meat. To refuse the squash was to refuse my parents' love.

And when I brought a man home for Sunday dinner, my father slyly watched him pass his plate to my mother for vegetables. A real man could get away with refusing potatoes or cauliflower, but not squash. Never the squash. For the first year of my first marriage, my father often called my husband Lawrence, which wasn't his name. I suspected it was because my husband refused the squash.

I would never have the space or need for all the varieties of winter squash my father grew. But I decided I had to have at least one kind to honour him, and it would be a butternut because there are so many ways to prepare it.

Tomatoes were really *the* vegetable — or fruit, I should say — that I wanted most in my garden. The sight of flourishing plants with fat, healthy tomatoes equals garden success to me. I'd been disappointed in my tomatoes the previous year. About the time my zucchini gave up, the leaves on my tomato plants had started to shrivel and turn brown. I knew I'd planted the tomatoes too close together and suspected that a single plant I'd bought at a plant sale had infected the others. As well, I'd made the mistake of growing the small Sweet Million tomatoes from seeds I'd collected. Then I'd learned the bitter truth: you can't grow hybrid tomatoes from your own seeds. The tiny tomatoes looked perfect but they tasted so awful I had to spit them out.

I would buy all new seeds for the tomato rows and choose disease-resistant varieties for my sauce and eating tomatoes, and when it came time to draw my rows on a map, I'd make sure to leave enough space for the Romas and Big Beefs I'd selected, so they wouldn't touch. And on my map, I'd draw the tomato rows where tomatoes hadn't grown in the past two years. For my pots on the deck, I'd choose cherry and patio tomatoes that promised abundance.

I have this, I told myself. Peter's surgery was happening. Recovery and my successful garden would come soon after.

Chapter Seven

THE NEXT STEP BEFORE ORDERING my seeds was to draw my maps to see how many vegetables I could fit in my beds. But as we got closer to Peter's big day, I thought about the garden less often. Then, the weekend before the Monday surgery, I got the first cold I'd had all winter and it knocked me out. I slept in the guest room so I wouldn't share my germs with Peter. Luckily, Jane was visiting that weekend and brought me cups of tea.

By the morning of the surgery, I felt stronger. Peter and I were ready to leave by 4:15 a.m. But I didn't want to leave the house quite that early. St. Joseph's Hospital was just an hour away, after all. The doors to the surgery's reception area wouldn't open until 6:00 a.m., and I didn't want Peter standing around. Or maybe I wanted to feel in control of something. That was a mistake. The worst snowstorm of the winter descended on us in the pre-dawn hours. Driving on the dark country roads that hadn't been ploughed and on the highway where dividing lines were invisible was treacherous and slow. I went as fast as I could, but drove with extra care and tried to lighten the tense mood in the car. "It would be a shame if I got us killed on the way to life-saving surgery," I

Debi Goodwin

said, and we both laughed a little at my joke. But that was the
only moment of humour on the trip. As time sped up and traffic
slowed, our anxiety grew. I didn't mind the snow so much, but my
night vision was not what it had once been, so keeping inside the
unmarked lanes took all the concentration I could manage. I tried
to ignore the niggling talk in my brain that the weather and the
fact we'd be late were signs the surgery wouldn't go well.

My unease continued throughout the morning. When we got
to the surgery wing, about fifteen minutes late, Peter was pulled
ahead of those with numbers who had duly arrived at six on the
dot. He had to be prepped for his eight o'clock surgery, so we had
to say goodbye too quickly.

I settled in for the wait, worried I'd start coughing and not be
able to stop. I had considered wearing a mask in the waiting room
but didn't, reasoning I was past the contagious stage of my cold.
Instead, I sucked on lozenges when I couldn't hold the coughs in
any longer. No one around me seemed concerned; everyone was
lost in a private bubble of worry.

The St. Joseph's Hospital surgery waiting room was pleasant and modern, with soft colours, big windows, and couches
that divided the long space into living room–sized areas. In my
"living room," I sat with an Italian Canadian woman whose husband was getting a new knee, a Peruvian Canadian woman whose
husband was losing a kidney, and a young Portuguese Canadian
man whose pregnant fiancée was having an ovarian cyst removed.
In a matter of minutes, we knew each other's stories, discussing
details that you'd share only with intimate friends or strangers
you'd never see again. We sipped from our Tim Hortons cups
and watched a computer screen that tracked the progress of our
loved ones.

One by one, surgeons came out and talked to the people in
my circle. One by one, each person left to visit their partner in a

bed somewhere. I stared at the wall clock and watched the minute hand move past the maximum time of three to four hours we'd been given for Peter's surgery. On the computer screen, Dr. F's next patient remained stuck in the "waiting for surgery" box and Peter stuck in surgery.

Outside, the snow was still falling — slushy stuff now that streaked the grey sky and spat on the windows. I tried to breathe. I tried to meditate, but the panic rose anyway. Jane had offered to take the day off work to be with me, but I knew that meant she'd lose a day's wages and her government employer didn't pay her enough as it was. But alone in the circle, I wished I hadn't persuaded her not to come.

The Peruvian Canadian woman came back from a walk; her husband was still in recovery and she was waiting to see what room staff would move him to. She had a friend with her and they talked quietly in Spanish. But seeing my distress, the friend asked me for my husband's name.

"Peter," I said, feeling each syllable leave my lips and my throat vibrate with emotion. It felt good to say his name aloud, making him alive and real in the space.

"We'll pray for him," she said.

It was a long Spanish prayer, unfathomable to me. But I let the words wash over me, felt the kindness of this stranger.

"*Gracias,*" I said when she finished.

"You're welcome," she answered.

After five hours, Dr. F emerged, looking weary. He signalled for me to follow him into a private space. Peter had come through the surgery fine, but the operation had been more difficult than Dr. F had believed it would be. Dr. F is no novice; he's considered a top-notch thoracic surgeon and works at both the provincial and federal level to promote esophageal cancer awareness. He said that it had been tricky working around Peter's scar tissue from previous surgeries, and to his surprise, the esophagus had been extremely close to the aorta. He hadn't been able to see that on the CT scan.

"I don't understand what you're saying," I said.

He took a pen out of his pocket and started drawing on the leg of his scrubs. His pen stopped working and I dug in my purse for another. With it, he drew two lines. He said he had to slice very carefully along the side of the esophagus so he wouldn't cut the aorta.

"I don't know if I got it all," he said. He then went on to talk about the woodiness of the tumour and how he'd had to burn the thoracic duct shut so it didn't bleed into the esophagus. That procedure would leave Peter prone to pneumonia. But really, all I heard clearly was "I don't know if I got it all." At some level, I knew I was listening to a surgeon's postgame musings, but as I left him I felt devastated nonetheless.

It would be a couple of hours before Peter's next move in the hospital would be posted on the monitor, a few hours before I could see him awake. I had time to eat and make calls. In the cafeteria, most of the food stations were shutting down after the lunch period. At the salad station, the man working behind the counter was packing all the fresh ingredients away in plastic containers. He seemed eager to end his shift, showed no interest in making a salad for a late customer. I stood watching him and wanted to yell, *Et tu, Mr. Salad Man? Don't you know I need my vegetables? Are you purposely trying to fuck up my fucked-up day?*

Instead, I wandered around the cafeteria looking for something I could eat, something that would fill the emptiness in my stomach but make me feel good about what I was putting there. Something with vegetables. Over at the grill, which was still open, people were lined up for burgers and fries. The station was clearly popular enough to remain open all day. I stood at the end of the line, wavering. Tempted. Fries were my failing. I could eat them anytime. But I knew I needed something fresh to get rid of the foul taste that had built up in my mouth from fear and cold coffee.

I circled the cafeteria again and settled finally on a slice of a vegetarian pizza that sat on a raised platter under a heat lamp. The slice was salty and greasy. I ate it too fast. The heaviness in my stomach left me feeling angry with myself. And more disappointed in the day.

After lunch and my calls, I found Peter in a bed in the surgical intensive care unit. He had tubes attached to machines all over his body. One tube snaked out of his nose. Since there was no food going into him, they had to draw the bile still being produced for digestion out of him. My undigested pizza felt like a lump in my stomach.

That evening, when Peter was awake, Dr. F came back. "Everything went fine," he said.

Before I could think of the effect of my words on Peter, I blurted out, "But you said you didn't get it all."

"Oh, I got it all," he answered. "I was just being paranoid."

I didn't know which version of the man to believe, the worn-out surgeon postsurgery or the one trying to reassure a patient with cuts and tubes everywhere.

Peter was one of the best communicators I knew. He liked to talk to all sorts of people and to email family and colleagues links to articles of interest to them, and was known on Facebook for his many thoughtful, sometimes silly, and often personal postings, which earned him hundreds of followers. As well as *The Third Phase* blog we took turns writing, he'd started a blog with the title of his memoir, *The Man Who Learned to Walk Three Times*. In the blog, he'd written about polio and mobility issues until he received his cancer diagnosis and began to record his thoughts about his treatments.

But in his days in the surgical intensive care ward, Peter didn't
have the energy or the interest to reach out to anyone. And I was
feeling too anxious to continue keeping friends and relatives up to
date, which prompted some to send me angry emails. Peter was
annoyed on my behalf, but I didn't want him to have to respond to
those he felt were being unfair to me. We agreed I'd send a quick
mass email and post something on Facebook. On February twen-
tieth, four days after Peter's surgery, I posted the following on his
page: "The doctors are pleased with Peter Kavanagh's recovery after
surgery. He's feeling positive but still too tired and encumbered
with tubes to write that next post. But he will. Soon. Thanks for
all the support we've received."

I, of course, made no mention of the surgeon's worries. Friends
were grateful for the post and relieved to hear that Peter had survived. It didn't take much to reassure people, and I was sorry I
hadn't thought to do it earlier.

The nine days after Peter's surgery when he remained in hospital were lost days when all I did was function. Our American
friends insisted I not drive back and forth to the house every day
and said they were sending me money for a hotel room. I had
driven home the night of Peter's surgery to a driveway that needed
to be shovelled in the dark and a cold, empty house. But my friend
A said caretakers often die in highway accidents because of the
stress they're experiencing. She was a doctor; she'd seen the evi-
dence. I accepted the offer and for a few nights walked to my hotel
room after Peter tired out, stopping to find something to eat on
the way there.

During the first days Peter was in intensive care, food became
something to stuff into my mouth. Pizza, grilled cheese, fries,
potato chips, they all went in without my having any awareness of
their taste. When I finally did come to my senses and realized —
again — that I needed healthy food to keep me strong enough to

cope and to care for Peter, I started to eat salads, soups, and simple egg dishes. The secret, I discovered, was to stay away from the hospital cafeteria. The place that was supposed to be healing Peter was making me sick. I discovered a coffee shop nearby that made good, wholesome food, and I camped out there whenever I could. It was on the ground floor of an old Hamilton house, decorated with mismatched chairs and tables, and was so much more relaxing than the cafeteria that I had to drag myself back to the hospital.

Both Peter and I hated being in hospitals; he had been in way too many in his life; I had too many memories of my grandmothers and parents, who all died in hospital wards. One of the reasons I always take care of myself is to avoid doctors and hospitals as much as I can. Ironically, I'd fallen in love with a man whose health meant I spent more hours in hospitals than I ever imagined I would.

One evening, when I did drive home from Hamilton, I stopped at a market store in my town and spotted Belgian endive. Each yellowish cone tinged with green was wrapped in brown paper, too precious to mingle with the other vegetables. That endive took me back to Dijon, France, where I'd spent one year as a university student. When I'd allowed myself the luxury of eating out, I'd always ordered the appetizer known as *crudités* — round piles of grated beetroot, carrots, and celeriac in mustard dressing arranged on a platter. In the best places there'd also be a serving of minced endive.

I bought two endives, and as soon as I got home I chopped them and mixed up a mustard dressing. Then I put the endive salad on a clean white plate and savoured each tart mouthful at the table where Peter I shared so many meals and games of backgammon. Comfort food that brought true comfort.

On postsurgery day six, Peter got his first mouthful, not of food but of a foul-tasting dye so that technicians could watch to see if the stitches inside him held. When he passed this swallow test, his reward was a salty chicken broth, a cranberry cocktail drink, and tepid tea. He never drank tea — he was a faithful coffee man — so he made do with the fruitish drink and the broth. And once he was ready for soft foods, the menu didn't get any better. When the dietitian came into his room one day to check on him, she noticed he hadn't finished his portion of Salisbury steak and boiled vegetables, and she expressed the concern he wasn't eating enough. Peter pointed out he didn't like beef and he didn't find the industrial food particularly tasty. And that I'd been bringing him muffins from home and coffee from my favourite spot since he'd been able to eat.

The dietitian didn't disagree with Peter's assessment of hospital food, but she was still afraid he wasn't getting enough nutrition. She decided that when he was released from the hospital, he should keep the feeding tube that had been inserted in his belly during surgery to get nutrition into him. Even after he'd started eating the small hospital meals, the nurses had continued to use the tube to supplement his calories with a liquid product. Peter was not pleased at the idea that the tube would go home with him, but he agreed to learn how to keep it clean and fill it because he wanted to get out of the hospital.

On the last Saturday in February, Peter got his wish to go home. During his final days in the hospital, he'd had a large room to himself with a wall-sized sunny window that overlooked the front of the hospital and the road beyond it. It was about the best room anyone could get in a hospital, but both of us couldn't leave it fast enough. Some of Peter's old impatience, which I recognized from his days of chronic pain, resurfaced as we waited for all the doctors and nurses who had to see him and sign off on his release before we could go.

Back home, he took to his favourite chair in the great room and savoured his first coffee from our machine. I took a picture of him pointing at his mug in victory and sent it to Jane.

For the first time in months, Peter and I both felt like life might get back on track. His esophagus was still sore from the surgery, but he could swallow again without feeling any obstruction. The tumour had left his body. He knew he'd have to find foods that were nutritious without being too filling and learn to eat smaller portions so he wouldn't overload his reduced stomach, but he felt he was up to the task. As he reached for a book, content to be home, I settled at the counter and opened the file on my Victory Garden project, which had sat on my desk since the days before Peter's surgery.

I took out the two pieces of paper where I'd drawn scaled-down versions of the garden beds and began to plot the rows of vegetables. As I pencilled in the rows, I kept in mind two principles I'd read about: the amount of space required by different plants and the need for plant rotation. Changing the position of plants in beds each year helps prevent disease and maintains a balance of nutrients in the soil. Different vegetables use up different chemicals and micronutrients, so growing the same vegetable in the same spot year after year means all those chemicals and micronutrients will become depleted. To be safe, once a vegetable has grown in a spot, it shouldn't be planted there again for four years.

The tomatoes were hardest to relocate. I knew where I'd planted them the last summer and where the previous owners had grown them one year earlier, but I had no idea where they'd been the year before that. I drew two rows where I was certain there hadn't been any tomatoes in the past two years and hoped the winter had killed any tomato virus in the surrounding soil. My beans, on the other hand, had added nitrogen to the soil where they'd grown, so I drew them in on the other side of the garden to do good there.

By the end, I had a map for the largest vegetable bed with a row across the back where I'd put a net for peas and cucumbers.

Nine rows ran out from the net toward the lawn. In the two rows for beans and dwarf curled Scotch kale, I'd plant radishes first, since they would be eaten before I needed to get the beans in and before the kale grew too big to overshadow them. And I split several rows in half to get more varieties for my harvest. One row would have pak choi for stir-frying along with several varieties of lettuce, which I would keep resowing through the season as I'd learned to do from my Victory Garden readings. Another row would be divided between Redstart peppers and Burpee's golden beets. I envisioned different kinds of chard in another row; it would be a colourful line of red, orange, and yellow stems with deep-green leaves. Carrots and purple beets would claim the next two rows. The cabbages I planned to start from seed and then grow through their first stages in pots on the deck could go in bare spaces in those rows. I left another row for experimentation with rapini and later broccoli, where I could also fit in some late cabbages. In the two tomato rows, which needed more space around them than other rows, I'd also grow arugula and early types of lettuce before the tomato plants grew tall.

The map of the second vegetable bed was easier. In the end with my garlic, I'd add onions and leeks. In the other end, I'd plant my zucchini and Waltham butternut squash in hills of soil.

Smiling, I glanced at Peter, who was deep in his book, and past him to the yard, which was green again after the blast of winter we'd had. And then I turned my attention back to my file and the business of filling in the forms for ordering my seeds. Each of the catalogues had shipping charges, so I decided to order all my seeds from three catalogues: Stokes, Heritage Harvest Seed, and Ontario Seed Company. Since part of the victory in a Victory Garden is keeping costs down, I chose most of the seeds from Stokes, which had the best shipping rates. I knew I was ordering more seeds than I needed, but reasoned I'd keep what I didn't use in the dark and cool basement room as an act of faith that I would be gardening the following year. In past years, I wouldn't have given that notion a second thought. There were a lot of acts of faith going around that winter.

With the maps drawn, the seeds ordered, and Peter home, I felt a satisfying sense of accomplishment. Days in the summer garden seemed a little closer, and that was all I wanted to think about that morning. But there was still the fragile process of turning seeds into seedlings, and Peter's lengthy recovery, ahead of us. The rows on the map seemed straight, the promise of the vegetables in the catalogue vivid, and Peter enjoying his Americano reassuring. As much as I wanted to live in the moment of those thoughts, I couldn't completely shake off my doubts and my fears. Gardening, like life, can be full of uncertainty and shocks. Cancer recovery could go off the rails. And even the thought of a juicy tomato could not drown out the voice in my head that repeated the doctor's words: "I don't know if I got it all."

Chapter Eight

SPRING, AS WITH SO MANY THINGS that year, came like a slap in the face. The mild winter and the kale that still grew in March had raised my expectations of getting my vegetables in early. But spring arrived cold and cruel. A hundred years ago, in the Niagara Region they'd have called it a *backwards spring*, the kind of spring that kills the tender tips of blossoms that dared to emerge in the first warmth. Certainly, my own dream of beautiful rows of vibrant plants by late May was nipped in the bud.

Our expectations had also been raised by Peter's surgery. During the months he'd forced himself to eat and had undergone toxic treatments, we'd held fast to the idea that if the surgical procedure cut out all the cancer, he'd be cured. But on that front, too, we had to face a fearful reality and a slow recovery. There was always the uncertainty over cancer cells that might still be lurking in Peter's body. He had an incision running down his chest that refused to heal. And he experienced difficulties with the adjustments he had to make to the changes in his body. One of those adjustments was learning to sleep at a thirty-degree angle to keep stomach acids from flowing freely into his remaining esophagus, because surgery had destroyed the "door" that used to keep them out. But all the methods he tried in order to stay at the correct angle through the night caused him pain. And now that he could taste food again, he sometimes ate more than he should, making him uncomfortable for hours. Victory still felt a long way off, and we were worn out from the first round.

I returned to the distraction of reading about my garden. I signed out all the books on vegetable growing and soil amelioration I could from my local library. I was drawn most to the ones that were heavily illustrated with photographs of plump tomatoes and tall climbing vines. Like I've said, I'm a sucker for luscious-looking vegetables. Whenever I'm in a hardware store and spin the rack filled with plant seeds, I want to buy them all and want my produce to look exactly like the pictures on the packets. It's a bit like the old joke from the movie *Educating Rita*, when a heavy woman with thin hair points at a photograph of Princess Diana and tells Rita, a hairdresser, "I want to look like that." Of course, transforming seeds into presentable vegetables is more doable than a miraculous makeover, but seed-packet photos and book covers never show rotted ends or leaves eaten by insects or yellowed with blight. In the early spring there's still hope that vegetables will come out just as they should: picture perfect.

I liked the books best when they reassured me that I knew what I was doing. For instance, when several books suggested pinching the suckers that grow in between the stems of tomato plants, I felt my head nodding in agreement. It's something I've always done ever since my father showed me how to do it as a child. Each time I get rid of a sucker I feel I'm giving the rest of the tomato plant a boost of energy. As an adult, in Toronto, I'd shared that information with a fellow backyard gardener, a friend, who followed my advice until she visited a farmer or a nurseryman, who told her to leave the suckers alone as they would produce tomatoes, too. I remember her laughing at how my father had done it wrong for all those years. I continued to pluck my suckers anyway, and each time I twisted one off, I found myself figuring out new comebacks in my head: *Yeah, well, maybe there'll be tomatoes eventually on those suckers but not in our gardening zone* or *Yeah, well, my father had more big, fat tomatoes than we knew what to do with.* Snappy repartee like that. I was continually surprised by how much my friend's comments rankled. So when I read again and again on those cold spring days that pulling off the suckers was sound practice, I found myself shouting in my head, *See, my dad was right. So there.*

I do realize how childish it all sounds. But two things I take seriously are my father's reputation as a grower and tomatoes. When I was in high school, I had no choice but to go to the only secondary school for the town of Grimsby and the outlying district where my father was the principal. As an authority figure, he was an alien to me. At school I avoided him, and when a new, cool hippie guy moved to Grimsby and asked me in the hallway if I was related to the principal, I said, "Sort of." I couldn't wait to finish high school and get away from the gossips who knew everything I did. One time, before I could get home from a date in nearby Hamilton, a busybody had called my father and reported that the boy I was with had smoked marijuana. Once.

In my teenage years, I even tried not to be seen with my father around town. I'll never forget — or forgive myself for — the look of disappointment on his face when, in grade nine, I announced I had no interest in our annual fall trip to gather hickory nuts on the escarpment. But during the summers, when my father walked the farm and vegetable patch in his striped T-shirt, dirty pants, Wellingtons, and farmer's tan, I had complete faith in his ability to grow anything. And eating his tomatoes picked after a hot day in the sun remains one of my favourite childhood memories.

If life were simple, the answers on whether to pluck suckers and how to come back from cancer would be clear. However, life is not simple. And the internet doesn't make it any easier. On the internet the way forward becomes muddier the more you read. What should a patient eat after esophageal surgery? Not completely sure. What kind of wedge should Peter sleep on to prop him up without pain? Not sure. Is it always right to pull the suckers off tomatoes? Apparently not.

I scanned dozens of sites for an answer to the sucker question that I could live with. I found one YouTube video with a photograph of a man standing on a ladder between his twenty-odd-foot-high cherry tomato plants. I had no ambition to grow giant plants, but I still thought reading the man's secrets might be informative. Many of his "secrets" (just he, people who buy his book, and the internet know them) were plain common sense, but when it came to his method of plucking the suckers off tomato vines, they were beyond anything I'd ever have the patience to attempt. He had some odd combination of taking off five suckers from the lower branches and six from the top, or maybe it was three from the top and twelve from the bottom. I didn't bother to bookmark the video. It was never going to happen.

Finally, by sifting through all the books and sites, I came to a method I could manage, and it had to do with the two kinds of tomato plants. There are *determinate* tomato plants, ones that grow to a specific size before they flower and set their fruit. They are the bush tomatoes like the variety of Romas I planned for one row and the patio tomatoes I'd grow in pots. It is best not to pull the suckers off these plants so they will have as much fruit as they are predetermined to have in the right conditions. Then there are the *indeterminate* varieties like the Big Beef tomatoes I'd put in another row, which will grow and grow and grow for as long as they can. They would need pruning, or they'd put too much of their energy into their branches and become ungainly. These I would sucker.

I don't know if my father knew the difference between determinate and indeterminate tomatoes. But likely he did. He had studied agriculture at the University of Guelph before going into teaching. It's possible he only let me loose on the indeterminate tomatoes, or that's all he grew since sauce tomatoes weren't part of our WASP diet. I'll never know, so I decided to hold my tongue with my friend (maybe) and *sucker* with my newfound knowledge.

The library books forced me to rethink some of my other plans. I had thought rotation and spacing were the only two principles I had to follow when I mapped out the arrangement of the plants in my larger bed. But the books soon convinced me I might have to adjust my map to include a third principle of grouping the plants according to their nutritional needs. And I would only understand exactly how to meet the needs of leafy plants versus root ones versus fruit-producing ones like tomatoes if I knew more about my soil. I thought of sending soil samples to the University of Guelph to be analyzed. I had no idea if my soil needed more nitrogen or more calcium, was too acidic or too alkaline. But with the coolness of March, the slow pace of Peter's recovery, and my own fatigue after the trying times of his surgery, I never got around to it. Another year, another Victory Garden, I told myself. Like Peter's postsurgery recovery, it was all getting too complicated. I gave myself a break, told myself that when I got around to planting the garden, I'd see if I could group some similar plants that I could feed together and still respect the principle of rotation, which seemed more important to me. In terms of the soil, I decided to go with the organic gardening books that said compost and other organic matter would build up the soil for all plants if done consistently. In the fall, I'd added a summer's worth of compost and bags of sheep and cattle manure to a bed that was already filled with organic matter, and I planned to add more when I prepped the beds before planting.

While I was reading books and letting myself off the hook, Peter was slowly coming back. He began to figure out the right portion size for his meals. It was a victory of sorts, because he did like eating again and discovered he had an appetite before each meal. And he continued to be able to swallow food and enjoy its taste without a problem. I could tell because he smacked his lips for the first time in months.

There were missteps, though. We went out for our first restaurant meal since the diagnosis, to a local gastropub. We went at lunchtime when Peter could eat small, but the tomato soup he chose was too creamy and too rich for him. While I scarfed down mussels and frites, I watched him struggle with the contents of a small white bowl. And at home, sometimes his appetite still got the better of him after months of food being something he had to choke down. With heaviness in his stomach and pain in his back, nights brought little rest.

Peter also had to face the truth about beer. He had been a connoisseur of craft beer for years, had become excited each time he found a new beer he liked during our travels. In India, he favoured Kingfisher, although he remarked that its slogan at the time, "Enjoyed by millions," didn't mean much in a country of more than a billion. In Vietnam, he drank fresh beer in Hanoi, a beer brewed each morning that only lasted a day. We even had a beer joke in Vietnam about two beers called Hue (pronounced "way") and Huda. "No Hue. Huda thunk it?" we'd say each time we found both brews in a restaurant. Whenever we drove to visit our American friends in upper New York State, we stopped at a small store where they sold Ommegang beer from Cooperstown. One year at Christmas I bought Peter the only variety of Ommegang I could find in Toronto, a stout in their *Game of Thrones* series, even though I knew it wasn't his favourite. But on Christmas morning I learned I'd scored big when he marvelled at the bottles I'd purchased. Apparently, in the States, thirsty drinkers were bidding high on eBay just to get one bottle of the stuff. And, after our move to Niagara, Peter was thrilled to discover that a local craft brewery, Silversmith, had some fine choices on tap.

A beer on a summer day on our deck equalled pure relaxation for Peter, whether it ended a week of long hours at the CBC or a day of pleasure reading. I can still see him on a summer evening at our old Toronto home pouring an Arrogant Bastard Ale into a chilled beer tankard and chuckling over its slogan, "You're not worthy." The only alcohol Peter liked more than beer was the Italian liqueur grappa, which he'd discovered on our first magical evening at Florian's in Venice as something to go with his double espresso.

But now he had to give up beer. It was just too filling for his much smaller stomach. I told him that maybe once he had his strength back, he could have a single beer for supper one night. But in the philosophical way he'd approached many of the limitations his health had forced on him, he shrugged the idea off. He'd have a white wine now and again; he'd learn to enjoy a glass of white wine. And there was still grappa.

It was harder for him to be philosophical about his difficulties sleeping. The first wedge we bought, made of thick foam by a company in Quebec, lifted his upper body to the angle he needed, but he was bent so sharply at the waist that he'd wake up with shooting back pain.

And the healing of his incision was frustratingly slow; we drove three times a week to a nursing centre in St. Catharines where they changed his dressing — a long, wide strip of gauze that ran from below his collarbone to his navel. Peter had never worn undershirts in his life before his cancer diagnosis. But he had that winter because he'd always felt cold. Now he wore them to keep the dressing in place. During a visit to the surgeon in March, the resident doctor seemed shocked at the rawness of the wound. In front of Dr. F, she suggested an antibiotic.

"Really," I said before I could stop myself, "he's just getting his gut in order." Dr. F told the resident an antibiotic wasn't necessary; the incision would heal.

On the matter of whether he had got all the cancer, Dr. F gave us mixed messages. "We'll get you right," he said one time. But during another clinic visit, he said he felt guilty — a strange choice of words, I thought — and he told Peter to do what he wanted in the next two years since there was only a 45 percent chance of a cure. When I asked what we could do to keep Peter in the cured group, Dr. F said there was nothing we could do. "Exercise, eat right, but don't bother with supplements because they don't work," he said.

Again, I felt frustration at being caught in the middle of conflicting information, more than in the trivial matter of how to sucker tomatoes. Doing what was right to keep Peter healthy was a matter of life and death. We had visited a cancer naturopath in December to see what foods and supplements might help. She was a caring, knowledgeable person with sound advice. The team at Juravinski hadn't been thrilled we'd gone to see her; we'd consulted with the oncologist on a couple of treatments the naturopath wanted to try. There's an infusion of large amounts of vitamin C, for example, that naturopaths say enters the cancer cells and kill them. The method has had some success in breast cancer patients. But oncologists don't want patients building up their immune systems, and they see vitamin C in those terms even if that is not the intent of the infusion. Dr. D, the chemo oncologist, didn't want Peter to do it. She cited one study on vitamin C infusions and one form of cancer that showed the infusions had done harm. We declined the infusion and the naturopath took it graciously.

We were, though, happy to follow the naturopath's nutritional suggestions that were based on science and studies. Peter drank aloe vera gel and swallowed calendula tablets to soothe his raw throat. She advised us to add black raspberries to Peter's diet; they are high in a compound called anthocyanin, which had proved effective in reducing esophageal tumours. Although I found the studies online, I could not find the freeze-dried black raspberries or black raspberry powder they referred to anywhere in Canada. Finally, I found a French black raspberry jam, sweetened only with grape juice, that I added to Peter's smoothies through the winter and spring. I drew black raspberry bushes on one side of my Victory Garden map and started searching for a nursery where I could buy the plants.

I understand that cancer doctors often dismiss the ideas of alternative medicine, not only for egotistic, "doctors are always right" kind of reasons, but also because they fear that desperate patients will try all sorts of unfounded treatments and end up like Steve Jobs, who, some believed, might have been saved by traditional cancer treatments. I also understand why natural healers worry about the toxic effects of established procedures like radiation and chemotherapy. I just wish the two sides would get their acts together and find some common ground so patients don't have to do it themselves at one of the most demanding times of their lives.

But even in the world of cancer doctors, there's confusion. After the surgery, Dr. F wanted to send Peter back to the radiologist, Dr. S, for more blasts in the region he'd had difficulty cutting out. Peter and I were both pretty sure Dr. S had told us he'd given Peter all the radiation he could without damaging organs. And when we did go back to the Juravinski, that's precisely what he told us. "You need your heart and lungs," Dr. S said.

Both he and the chemo oncologist, Dr. D, seemed pleased with the results of the pathology report. The cancer in the lymph nodes was gone. The cancer had made it into the muscle of the esophagus — who knew it had one? — but they saw no reason to believe Dr. F hadn't got all that. And until scans showed otherwise, there was nothing they could do.

But Dr. D did say, "Cancer is a tricky disease. If it comes back, it's usually in the first two years." We would have to wait until a CT scan in late May to see if the cancer was indeed gone before doctors would do a single thing more.

Still, we tried to keep our minds on victory, and, for me, thinking about my garden helped. Early in March two parcels of seeds arrived at the post office. In our town we had to pick up our mail, and during the eighteen months we'd been there, I'd painstakingly established a rapport with a woman who worked behind the counter, a woman with a sarcastic bent and what seemed like disdain for the new retirees who'd made the postcard town their home. I handed her two cards that had been left in our box and she found the matching packages in the backroom. As she gave them to me, she noticed the logos for the seed companies. "You're optimistic," she said.

"Yes, I am," I told her. I thought I saw a glint of new respect, a twinkle that said, *So you're not just another big-city retiree*, but I might have imagined it.

Once I had the seeds, I tried to decide the timing of when to start germinating them so the plants would be the right size at the right moment. Some varieties needed four weeks, some six, before they could be set out after the last frost. Traditionally, in my family, the Victoria Day weekend was considered the first safe weekend to plant tomatoes and other tender plants. But the earth had warmed since my grandparents' days and I'd found I could safely put out most plants a week or two before the holiday. But would I be able to this year, with its miserable spring?

The year before, I'd started seeds on windowsills. But I decided with a Victory Garden, I'd set up a system with lighting in the basement. I bought two fluorescent grow lights and a frame to hold them that would hang from the joists in the ceiling. But the lamps sat in their packages for weeks. The weather, like Peter's slow recovery, was holding us back. Snowfalls in early April deepened my inertia and kept me from getting outside to get the vegetable beds in shape. It was time to plant radishes and lettuce, but I just couldn't get started.

The second weekend in April, with the weather still unseasonably cold, I started my tomato and basil seeds indoors. A week later, I started zucchini, red pepper, broccoli, and Armenian cucumber. I set them all in front of bright windows and started to assemble the lighting system for their second stage, when their true leaves emerged. I did this without my usual enthusiasm for the first step of the season; I was starting to have doubts the seeds would grow or my garden would flourish. Maybe I was still too scared to believe Peter would be all right, so I couldn't imagine anything would turn out as it should.

One Sunday smack dab in the middle of April, when I usually had my early vegetables in, I got T to come for the day to help me get the vegetable beds ready. I'd found T the year before through friends in town. He was a young man who loved the earth, a guy who lived from day to day by working where he could. Once, the previous spring, when I'd hired him for two days in a row, I said I'd pay him the second day. But he asked for his payment for the first day right away so he could buy supper that evening. It was only then I realized how close he lived to the line.

There was something hapless about T that made people in town watch out for him. At a small restaurant where locals go, the bartender once gave him twenty dollars for a haircut. Peter and I assumed he hadn't used the money for the cut since his hair looked as though someone had put a bowl on his head and cut around it. But I trusted T and found him to be an efficient worker, so proud of his work he'd take pictures with his phone of trees he'd planted.

With T the year before I'd planted cedars, yews, and a hemlock tree; prepared the vegetable beds; and pulled out deep-rooted grasses to plant Japanese maples and perennials. And I'd had him move rocks for me. In Toronto, I'd created a rock garden with flats of rocks and found rocks. Over a ten-year period, I'd moved the garden up our sloped front yard until all the grass was gone, replaced by rocks, ground cover, and perennials. But I'd also done a lot of harm to my lower back, ending up in the emergency ward one time when I couldn't stand up straight. In this garden, I promised myself, I wouldn't do further damage. When I had rocks to move and large trees to plant, I called on T, who is a very big guy.

As he was moving one rock to a place under a tree, he complained that people thought of him as just a heavy lifter. I held my tongue because it was true. But, in a strange way, I liked his company. He talked continuously about his troubles with women, the temporary shelters he'd lived in — barns, basements, greenhouses — and the places in this tourist town where local workers could get a good deal on a decent meal. I also learned a lot from him about the nursery and farming businesses in the area. But more than that, we shared a love of dirt and growing things.

Peter often prepared tea for us to drink while we worked. One time he called us to the deck to get our cups and T just sat down and, without a single question from Peter, ranted about the sorry state of his love life for forty minutes while I got back to work in the garden.

One of the reasons I worked alongside T was to keep him focused. He had a dreamy state of mind and could get lost in studying the lines on a fallen nut or the trails of worms moving in the dirt. But he also could work fast and I had to keep coming up with new tasks for him. T had come to the region from northern

Ontario to study horticulture at Niagara College; he'd dropped out to work in a greenhouse, which then failed. His passion was terraforming — creating self-sustaining landscapes — and he wanted someday to practise that on a plot of land. In the fall, he'd run into a man from Australia who was working on terraforming projects there and invited him to come to work with him. T had thought he might head to Australia in January, but was worried about leaving the life he'd established here.

"Go," I'd told him. "You're young. Have an adventure."

So when I phoned him in April to see if he was around, I was surprised to get him on the first call. "Did you go to Australia?" I asked.

"Not yet. I don't have a passport. I'm still working on it."

He agreed to come that Sunday to help dig the vegetable beds. We began by pulling up the still-live kale plants so we could layer organic matter on the whole bed. I picked all the fresh leaves I could from the plants before tossing them in the compost, and I gave T a bag of baby kale.

"Wow, and it's organic," he said.

Over the winter he'd given up smoking, found cheap yoga classes in town, lined up a new girlfriend, and got a better haircut. The yoga had made him lean, the young woman had made him happy, and his newfound love of all things healthy had made him a cautious eater. When I offered him the milky Earl Grey tea he'd welcomed the year before, he said he was worried about the hormones in the milk and asked for green tea instead. When we raked off the straw I'd spread on the beds in the fall, he discovered some of it had sprouted in the mild winter and he eagerly picked the grassy shoots to make juice. "Do you know how much they charge for one of those drinks?" he said. But then he decided the straw I'd bought might be genetically modified and threw all the green stems away.

We got a lot done that day, covering the bed with steer and duck manure, as well as a sea compost that T said would add a lot of micronutrients. By the afternoon, both beds were ready for planting, but I knew I wouldn't get to it anytime soon. The weather was still cold, and I'd come to understand the vegetable garden had more to do with my sense of victory than Peter's. It wasn't just that he'd never had as much fondness for vegetables as I did; he'd never shown an inclination to drop a seed in the ground. It was time to shift my focus in the garden.

Trees had always given Peter joy. And getting more of them into our garden would be his act of faith. His love of trees began when he was in that body cast as a boy and stared at a tree outside his window for a whole year. He'd been in awe of its changes while he lay still in a bed at the back of his family's house. And so, while we waited for the weather to warm and Peter to feel stronger, the two of us came up with a plan to add as many trees as we could that spring. We drove to the best nursery in town and picked out a weeping pine for the backyard and, for a redesigned front yard, a yellow magnolia, a second flowering dogwood, and a Japanese red maple.

As we walked around the nursery with the woman who was helping us with the changes to the front yard, we stopped at a row of red maples. There were several short and cheaper trees to choose from and one tall, elegant one with a long curving branch that was, of course, double the price.

"Let's get that one," Peter said.

"Good choice," the woman from the nursery said. "That way you won't have to wait as long for it to grow."

Neither Peter nor I said anything, but I knew that we were both thinking that if Peter saw that tree grow to its full twenty feet, it would be a major victory for him.

The next time I had T over, I had him dig up the deep roots of a large grassy plant to make space for the weeping pine. I told him we were going to have a landscaper plant the other trees even though we didn't know how long we'd be in this house. I'd told T that Peter had been sick over the winter, and in the way of small towns, T already knew all about the cancer, but seemed happy to let the subject drop. That day as he dug the hole for the pine tree, he said, "I think it was Thomas Jefferson who said, 'If I knew I was going to die tomorrow, I'd still plant an apple tree today.'"

It wasn't Jefferson, I discovered later. The quote has been attributed to Martin Luther in this form: "Even if I knew that tomorrow the world would go to pieces, I would still plant my apple tree." But T had captured the way Peter and I planned to approach life and our garden.

Near the end of April, when radish leaves should have been pushing through the soil, I still hadn't planted their seeds or any seeds for lettuce or the early peas. Working on the tree and flower beds and waiting for the weather to warm had held me back. My Victory Garden was off to a very slow start.

But indoors, my tomato seedlings had their first true leaves and were getting larger each day. I had transplanted them into bigger pots and set them under the grow lights. I loved looking at them. All I had to do to imagine summer and the red fruit I'd pluck from the vines was wander down into the basement and marvel at the plants' leaves, which were almost translucent under the florescent light. I'd run my hand over the small leaves, because I'd read that was a good way to familiarize them with the feel of the wind, and say, "Soon, tomatoes. Soon, we'll all be outside and thriving."

Chapter Nine

WHEN IT CAME TO VICTORIES, early May brought few on the gardening and healing fronts. The weather — fickle friend that it is — finally came through, first with one beautiful weekend for Mother's Day. Jane came to visit from Toronto, and she immediately volunteered to help in the garden. But I didn't want her to spend all weekend working. Hell, *I* didn't want to spend all of the first beautiful spring weekend working.

On Saturday morning, Peter was content to take advantage of the warmth and sit outside on the deck to read and admire the garden, but Jane craved a walk in a woods. I suggested an intriguing trail I'd noticed off the Niagara Parkway. Jane and I followed a path through budding trees to a lookout over the Niagara gorge, the swirling turquoise water far below us — a wild, natural view marred only by the buildings of a resort across the way and a helicopter taking tourists on a ride over the whirlpool and nearby falls. When the helicopter disappeared, leaving a trailing buzz behind it, large birds — hawks or eagles, I didn't know which — took its place high in the sky and then slowly circled downward. It was like being in the opening of a political thriller, with the distant buzzing a tension track and the hawks a cinematographer's symbol of a shock to come. As more and more birds — at least six, maybe ten — dropped closer to us, I got spooked.

It didn't take much to spook me that spring. Waiting for a date for Peter's first postsurgery CT scan, waiting to get out in the garden, had left me fragile, easily pushed over the edge into a mush of primitive emotions.

Usually, I love birds. The ones that swooped through our wide, open backyard delighted us both. But these ones managed to vibrate old fears in me, like a finger pinging a tuning fork. When I was a girl, my mother had been so terrified of birds she'd scream whenever one got into our house down the old brick chimneys, which happened more often than you might think. My father would chase the frantic, flapping bird out with a broom while my sister and I both yelled at him not to hurt it. Years later, when I discovered Margaret Laurence's *A Bird in the House* and learned of the superstition that a bird in the house was an omen of death, it seemed to echo my mother's terror. And then I watched Alfred Hitchcock's *The Birds* late one night as a teenager and, well, that didn't help any.

In my practical way, I knew I'd be afraid of birds forever if I didn't do something, so when I went to Europe for my year of study and visited London on my way to France, I purposely stood in Trafalgar Square, stretched out my arms, and let the pigeons, which were so plentiful in that square, land on me. I tensed at first, but eventually relaxed as I realized nothing terrible was going to happen. And I took that as a lesson: facing fears is always better than harbouring them. Still, out in the woods that day with my mind in constant anxiety over Peter, I realized those childhood memories still resided deep in my bones. And there was nothing practical I could do to eliminate my fears about Peter. The Victory Garden was as close as I could come.

I told Jane I wanted to move on, and we soon discovered another path that led to rough timber and earth steps down to a climb over rocks and finally to the bottom of the gorge. Fear and worry flew from me as they so often do when I walk in nature. We rested by the swirling waters and watched fishers cast their lines. My mind, now calm, returned to the necessities of my garden. I eyed rocks beside us that would look good at home. Ever since I'd left my vast collection of rocks behind in our Toronto garden, I'd found the beds at the new house rather barren before the plants came up. I picked through the rocks in the woods until I found one that had beautiful markings in green and red, one that wasn't too heavy to carry. After I wrapped it in my sweatshirt to take home, Jane said I was crazy to haul it to the car but insisted on carrying it up the stairs.

That afternoon, with the rock placed in a new spot in the garden, Jane and I decided to do some work. I cleared branches, twigs, and leaves from the flower beds while Jane took on the task of picking up plugs from the lawn. Peter and I thought we'd been smart to have the lawn aerated, not realizing the machine the landscaper used would leave plugs of hard earth that looked like small cigars all over the grass. Jane became obsessed with getting them all up, moving across the lawn on her hands and knees while she listened to the newest Beyoncé album through earphones connected to her phone.

With the light fading, I had to keep calling her to stop and join Peter and me on the deck. I told her the remaining plugs would eventually break down in the rain, but on Sunday morning she went back out, criss-crossing the lawn.

I decided it was time to get the Victory Garden officially started. In the fall, I'd bought a kit for a net on sale to set up in the larger vegetable bed to support the peas and, after the last frost, the Armenian cucumbers. But when I opened the retaped box, I discovered key elements were missing, including the netting pictured on the front. I'd have to take the kit back and figure out some other arrangement. I took some iron posts the former owner had left behind and Jane held them while I stood on a ladder and pounded them into the ground; they would support the netting that I'd buy when I could. I didn't want to plant the peas or the rows of greens in front of the peas until that netting was in place. Another delay.

A few days later, I did buy the netting, along with some raspberry bushes, sets of leeks for Peter, and some heirloom tomato plants at a local plant sale. It was too early for the leeks and tomatoes, but it felt good to plant the berry bushes, including a black raspberry bush I'd found, to finally get something in the ground. But when I started to set up the pea net, I realized I was short a pole to hold the full length up. Yet another delay.

The annoying holdup in getting the vegetables planted was nothing compared to the continuing frustration Peter felt over the surgical wound on his chest that still required a fresh dressing every few days. Each time I drove him to the nursing centre in St. Catharines where they took care of him, he came out looking dispirited. The different nurses he encountered tried to reassure him the incision was healing, though slowly because of his age and the effects of the radiation and chemo. But their reassurances did little. Peter wanted the wound healed and he wanted the scan over with. He wanted his life back.

In the meantime, while I waited for soil to warm and Peter waited for skin to knit, we turned our attention again to our trees. We got pruners in to clean up some of the older trees in our backyard and took the opportunity to get rid of an ugly old ornamental blue spruce that stood like a blob next to our deck, blocking the view of half our garden.

But by the middle of May I was eager to turn all my gardening attention to the Victory Garden. I wanted to get seeds into the ground, to start us moving into a new season of growth and abundance. The weather, however, had a different plan. The forecast for our region for May fifteenth called for flurries and freezing temperatures. On Twitter, someone from Burlington wrote, "Wanted: Mother Nature. Offence: Theft of Spring. If located, do not approach, lately been very unstable. Possibly running with Old Man Winter."

Despite the cold, I had to get something done. The softly turned, unplanted vegetable beds felt like a recrimination. By this time the year before, I'd already had healthy young plants in neat rows and was picking small greens for salads. So I had Peter come out and hold a pole that I'd discovered in the back of the shed while I pounded it into the ground. Then I tied the rest of the pea mesh to the last pole and wove four bamboo stakes through as crosspieces. Some drops of rain fell as I scooped out two trenches on each side of the mesh wall. But I didn't let that stop me. I was determined to get something started. The planting directions on the packet were confusing, and in my haste to get the job done before I got too cold, I simply turned to my old method of using my gloved thumb to poke holes in the shallow trenches and place the peas approximately the right distance apart. They lay there round, hard, and inert, but I knew that with a little rain, a little sun, they would do what peas in the ground did and new plants would emerge. I slapped the earth over them with satisfaction. I had finally begun.

Meanwhile, inside the house, under the grow lights, my tomato seedlings were transforming into healthy plants with thick stems and strong secondary leaves. Beside the tomato plants, I'd set a few Redstart peppers, broccoli, rapini, and basil seedlings, which all looked promising, too. Those were all the surviving seedlings I had.

We'd gone away in late April on a road trip through northern New York State to Pittsburgh, a surprisingly vibrant city. The trip was the right thing to do. Earlier, at a visit to the surgeon, Peter had asked when he could travel. He was impatient to make up for lost time, to normalize his life again. And that trip to Pittsburgh gave him a feeling of freedom and sense of recovery.

On our first day we stopped at Letchworth State Park, an area of valleys and trees we'd always wanted to visit. We stood at a lookout and watched birds swoop across the gorge. When a park police officer came up beside us, he identified which birds were turkey vultures and which were eagles. Peter told the man he had a wonderful place to work. The officer answered that his job had its drawbacks and described being part of the search for a boy who had gone off the trail and fallen over the edge. We all stared at the steep slope to one side of us, where there was nothing to stop a fall. The officer had been part of the team that had walked through the waters of the Genesee River below to find the body so that a helicopter could airlift it. The death had occurred more than a year earlier but the officer still looked haunted. Perhaps he always would.

From the park we drove to the small town of East Aurora, where we'd booked a room at the refurbished Arts and Crafts building now known as the Roycroft Inn, a place we'd loved to stay at in our Toronto years. Peter was too tired to explore restaurant possibilities in the town, but he didn't want to eat in the inn's dining room either, as he felt he'd have to order a main dish with too much food for him. Instead, we went into the lounge. We were the only guests there and happily lingered over a meze platter and wine. In the way travel teaches us things, we learned a valuable lesson that night about managing food on the road that gave both of us the confidence to consider longer trips once Peter had a first clear scan. Just being happy together in that beautifully restored room strangely boosted our belief that the scan would be clean.

In Pittsburgh, Peter seemed his old self, even if we had to keep the days short so he could rest. He'd spent some of his early working years in Sydney, Nova Scotia, where his parents then lived. He had an affinity for steel towns, and loved seeing how Pittsburgh, like many steel towns in North America, had transformed itself, drawing visitors with its Andy Warhol Museum and its thriving restaurant scene. Zagat had recently named Pittsburgh the number one food city in America.

Peter had always wanted to write a book about grappa. When we'd been guests at two famous distilleries, Nonino and Poli in northern Italy, the owners had been impressed by his knowledge and enthused by the idea of a book that would share the feminist history of artisanal grappa. Peter was thrilled to discover he could get back into his research in Pittsburgh, giving him renewed interest in his project. Online, he'd discovered a bar there called Grapperia, which served grappa and grappa cocktails, and a distillery called Wigle that had once bottled its own grappa. He made appointments at each place and recorded interviews on his iPad. I was thrilled to watch him asking his intriguing questions, being recognized for his smarts and wit.

I was especially touched when he connected to the young man who had opened Grapperia a year earlier. Domenic Branduzzi had created the bar as a tribute to his Italian father, who had taught him to appreciate grappa. It was clear this man was still hurting from the loss of his father. Peter rarely told strangers he had cancer, but he did tell Domenic, who offered up his favourite grappa cocktails and sat with us at a table in his small bar long after the interview had ended.

Peter also seemed to get over his fear of going into restaurants at dinnertime while we were in Pittsburgh. From the bar, we went on to Piccolo Forno, Branduzzi's family restaurant, where Peter ordered gnocchi (a favourite dish) and nothing else. And he ate it all.

The next night it was so warm in the city, we decided to eat outdoors at a restaurant Peter had read about. The late evening sun shone on us as our huge portions of food arrived. Peter could only manage half of his chicken dish, so we wrapped the other half up. We had a cooler in the car, and he ate the rest the next day for lunch at a roadside stop. These are the kind of details most people would quickly forget, but they were huge steps for us, successes on the way to victory.

In gardening terms, the trip came with a trade-off. I lost half of the seedlings I'd started before we'd left. I'd given my neighbour poor instructions on how to keep them moist, had told her a squirt of water each day would be enough out of fear she'd overwater. My Armenian cucumbers and all my squash seedlings were dried out stems when I got home. It was too late to start germinating another round inside; I'd have to grow the plants directly from seed in the garden, which would make for a later crop. As with anything that matters in life, you can't take your eye off emerging seeds.

When I was getting up from my knees after planting the peas that cold day in May, a toad hopped by me and I cheered silently so I wouldn't scare it off. We'd spotted their warty brown presence the year before and had, earlier in the spring, set out two toad houses to encourage them back into our yard. Unlike birds in houses, toads in gardens were good omens. They would eat insects, including mosquitoes — up to one hundred a day each — and in so doing, help keep our garden comfortable long into summer evenings. Despite shivers from the cold, a warm image flashed through my mind of Peter and me dining on the deck as the sun set late on a summer evening with the crickets as the only soundtrack.

The next day, I got out my map of the large vegetable bed and looked at how I could adjust it to group similar plants together while still honouring the principles of rotation. I started on the left side, setting up the teepees I'd created out of my father's old iron tomato rods for the Kentucky Wonder beans I'd plant after the last frost. In between the teepees, where the bush beans would later go, I planted radish seeds, since they would produce their sharp-tasting roots quickly. In the next row, I planted the kale seeds I'd chosen, interspersed with more radish seeds. Just as I'd planned. As I moved across the garden, I stuck pretty much to the original map, although I ended up putting the beets all together.

As I worked, I sang the words, at least the ones I could remember, to "What a Wonderful World." I had bookmarked it on my computer and, the evening before, I had watched Louis Armstrong sing it as a pep talk, just as I had many times during Peter's treatment.

I skipped over the rows for the tomatoes; it would be weeks before I could set them in the ground without the fear of frost killing them. Before that, in any case, I had to harden the seedlings, bring them out on the deck to acclimatize to strong sun and cool breezes. In two days, the temperatures were supposed to rise, and I'd start to carry the trays out for a few hours at a time, leaving them first in the shade. Then slowly, I would give them more hours of direct sunlight each day. If I rushed that process, the sun would burn the virgin leaves. Once the plants were tough enough, I'd leave them out overnight.

As I packed up my garden tools for the morning, I eyed how much space I had left in the garden and where the rows of eating tomatoes, chard, carrots, and later beets would go. It was going to be a very good garden.

After lunch that day, Peter and I drove out of town to visit a woman we'd recently met. JA was a local champion of the Jamaican migrant workers in the region. Earlier that spring we'd gone to a concert she'd arranged to welcome the workers back for another season. A gospel choir from Toronto had got the crowd out of their seats, clapping and dancing in the aisles. JA lived in a rambling house that was part bed and breakfast and part home. But it was her garden that captivated me. The garden, with a back-to-the-land seventies feel, had chickens in an outdoor pen and several beds for vegetables, with rows of vibrant rhubarb all ready to be picked. Over rhubarb crumble, we talked about the situation of the migrant workers. It was the fiftieth anniversary of the program that brought Caribbean and, later, Mexican workers to Niagara for the growing season, and JA wanted Peter's advice about telling their stories.

To my delight, Peter, the guy who loved big cities with all their bookstores, coffee shops, and energy, the guy who didn't have any one place he considered his childhood home, had taken to our new community as much as I had. Because of his father's work as a project manager on big construction jobs, Peter had lived in several provinces by the time he was fourteen and believed he could live anywhere. But the Niagara landscape seemed to resonate with him. On our many drives, we passed vineyards and orchards of peach and cherry trees and were both mesmerized by the sensation of row after row that seemed to be passing the car as we moved forward on the empty back roads. We crossed the deep swath of the Welland Canal and were rarely annoyed when we had to stop at a bridge to watch a towering ship appear to cross the road. And we remarked on the colours of the trees on the distant escarpment as they changed from the first yellow tips to a sea of green. It touched me to think Peter had finally found a true home, especially in a geographical area that so spoke to me.

My work on a committee that was bringing Syrian refugee families to the region was the one activity I did to feel part of the community. But Peter, who never did anything halfway, had, for a time, been involved with the Rotary Club and its campaign against polio through his book on his own experiences. Throughout his cancer treatments, he was a volunteer on one committee trying to get a World Heritage designation for the region and another to create a park from lands that had been used by the Department of

National Defence as a rifle range. That board wanted to preserve the last stand of Carolinian trees on the Great Lakes in a wooded area next to the range — trees that connected Niagara to vegetation farther south than most of Ontario could tolerate — as well as provide locals needed access to the lake. It also hoped at that time to see the different layers of the history of Niagara presented in the park with a small military museum and a healing garden to be created by a local Indigenous group in their fight against diets that had created so much diabetes in their people. Peter loved the idea of that park, and through his love of it, I could see his return to the calm he said he'd discovered watching that tree outside his window as a boy.

As the light stretched longer on suddenly glorious May days, I moved through the garden, adding strawberry plants, cleaning flower beds, and trimming bushes. Now that I had my first rows of vegetables in, I felt more relaxed, and I worked in my old rhythm of doing whatever I saw needed doing. I wanted the whole garden to be beautiful that year; it had filled us with peace and awe in our first summer and I wanted it to nourish our souls that year, just as the vegetables I was growing would nourish our bodies.

As I worked, I recognized something of my nature, of the distracted way I have moved through life. Friends often admire how much I get done, and I guess I do accomplish a lot. But I tend to lose focus, get easily bored, and switch to something else. And, that spring, I needed distraction more than ever.

We had a date for Peter's CT scan: May twenty-sixth. Then we'd have a week's wait for the results. I welcomed the firmness of a specific date; I'd felt a little like an airplane in a holding pattern ever since Dr. F had said he didn't know if he'd cut out all the cancer. Perhaps that is why the hovering birds had struck so much fear in me.

In my own need to move forward, I had agreed to go on a press trip to Andalusia, Spain, for a travel article. The trip would just take six days in late June, and Peter encouraged me to get back to the kind of work I loved to do in my semi-retirement: writing about my impressions of new places and photographing them. And I would get to see Alhambra, the Moorish palace that I'd always thought of as mystical but had yet to visit. I also hoped to add a weekend to the trip to visit a friend of mine who was teaching in Casablanca. I'd only have to pay for the hour flight from southern Spain, but I didn't want to commit to buying a ticket until I knew the results of the scan.

Peter, too, sought distractions in his writing and program of reading. He finally got back to his blog. He called his first post since his surgery "Seeking the New Normal." In it he described our trip to Pittsburgh, an evening we'd had in Toronto where he'd enjoyed appetizers at the Royal York's Library Bar, and then one bowl of soup that showed how his experiences with eating had improved so much.

A couple of nights ago I had a bowl of potato garlic soup, which was incredible. I loved the flavour, the texture, the taste. The fact that it was a small bowl was of little consequence. The wine I had with the soup was crisp, tart, cold, and a bit too expensive, but I am not complaining…. My surgeon says, I tell people [to] spend the first few years doing the things you most like doing. It is a plan.

So, the new normal? Figuring out what a decent-sized meal really is. Finding wines I really like. Reading books that matter and appeal to me. Talking with and spending time with people I truly enjoy. Writing what matters to me. Travelling with Debi wherever we can and whenever we can. Being with and content in the moment. This is the new normal.

While I gardened, Peter worked at finding his new normal. On his Facebook timeline, the new normal often involved food and quiet moments in the garden. "The new normal," he posted one night, "is at times a jumble. This evening salmon, wine and the sound of a dozen species of birds ... and solar lamps." Another time he wrote, "So today in my new normal, I mowed the lawn, smashed two solar lamps in the process, while Debi worked on the front rock garden.... I destroy, she creates, but then again I get to sip wine and enjoy her work. The new normal is great."

Many of Peter's Facebook followers responded with kindness and with thanks for reminding them to live in the moment. Others wanted more pictures of the garden or his recipe for the banana black walnut muffins he posted after he'd baked a batch.

Before discovering he had cancer, Peter had got a permit to drive, the first step in getting his Ontario licence. When he'd come from Halifax to work at CBC in Toronto in 1989, he didn't bother to change his licence, because he loved living in the city and walking about. He had never enjoyed driving, saw no reason for getting a car. He liked the idea of subways and trains. Over our years together, that had meant I'd been the only driver on our long driving trips in the States and Italy. And when I was ill, it meant I had to drive myself to the doctor, sometimes resenting the number of times I'd taken him to hospitals and doctors. Recognizing that I wanted a break from driving from time to time, he'd promised over the years to get his licence, but it wasn't until we moved to Niagara-on-the-Lake that he'd begun the process.

That spring, as he sought his new normal, he asked to go driving with me. He was a good driver, cautious but confident, and I enjoyed seeing the country roads around us from the passenger's perspective for the first time in years. One day I had to have drops in my eyes for an examination, drops that made the sun too bright for my dilated pupils and made driving difficult.

Peter drove me to the appointment and home again. "One down. Five hundred to go," he said, referring to all the appointments I'd taken him to.

And then he bought himself a small drone and practised flying it over the backyard. "OK, in today's version of finding the new normal, I bought a drone," he posted on Facebook along with an aerial shot of the garden. "So now I'm learning to drive a car, fly a drone and discover the new equilibrium all at the same time."

I watched him from the garden as he stood on the deck trying to control the drone's flight from his iPad. Before he got the hang of it, I ducked whenever the drone flew too low and then crashed. One video Peter recorded has an image of me scowling mysteriously up at the sky.

The week I got the first rows of vegetables in, I woke one night with a panic attack only a vegetable gardener can experience. An arugula panic attack. In other years, I'd planted the seeds for the peppery green as soon as the ground was soft or I had watched new plants emerge where seeds had naturally fallen. But I'd dug up my garden too early that spring to allow plants to take hold on their own and I hadn't planted any arugula seeds yet. The next morning, I got up early and sowed the seeds I'd collected from plants in the fall, and later, when I took Peter to the nursing centre, I bought a packet of arugula seeds in a nearby store so I wouldn't be without the possibility of planting more.

Later that day, we drove to Niagara Falls, New York, to pick up a new wedge for Peter's side of the bed. This one was available only in the United States and had a gentle incline that ended with a supporting layer for the torso. We hoped it would be easier on Peter's back than the first Canadian wedge we'd bought. Luckily, Peter had established an American postal address with a service on the other side of the border so we could easily pick up mail and books on our trips to the States.

Driving back toward Canada with the wedge in the trunk reminded me of a long-time familial connection to the region, one not related to orchards and gardens. For generations, my family had been going to Buffalo to shop for the day, just as so many people along the border did and still do when the dollar gap isn't too wide. One of my strongest childhood memories is of travelling with my sister and parents on a shopping expedition. Each girl wore a set of old clothing over the border which we replaced with a new outfit purchased to wear back. But underneath our outfits we both wore girdles for my mother. As a teenager, my mother had suffered from polio, which had damaged her back muscles. Despite warnings from doctors that childbearing would put too much stress on her back, she'd had five pregnancies, with four live births. To support her weakening back muscles as she aged, she wore a stiff one-piece girdle/bra set unavailable in Canada. My parents were hard-working, honest people, except when it came to smuggling necessities across the border. Just as my mother's need for those girdles cancelled out my parents' moral qualms, Peter's need for a wedge that might give his back some relief quashed mine.

On the way home, we stopped at the shop of a local potter who also kept bees. As I paid him for a jar of honey, we talked about the cold spring and how it was holding back our gardens. I told him I didn't know when I could get my tomatoes in and he gave me a tip: when the lilacs bloom, sensitive plants can go in the ground. This was a welcome bit of information for my collection of local lore. Earlier, I'd been told to prune the roses when the forsythia blooms. In the days of climate change, when the usual dates for planting are so unpredictable, tricks like these make a lot of sense.

While I waited for any sighting of pea sprouts, I added more evergreens to the back garden: euonymus along a fence, boxwood and a thin, twisting cedar to replace the fat blue spruce. And I divided perennials to fill in holes in the front. With T, I dug triple mix into all the flower beds before covering them with hemlock mulch. Meanwhile, my seedlings were resting under the shade of our deck's canopy before I allowed them to go into the sun, which was now strong and harsh. And I remembered how much I love May. So much happens in the garden in May. What I do in the garden in May sets the stage for the summer. It is the most hopeful of times.

Chapter Ten

THE WEATHER THAT SPRING switched so fast, we went from snow in the middle of May to a heat wave less than ten days later. While I welcomed the hot days, which meant summer would surely come and the ground would warm up to encourage all my seeds to sprout and reach for the light, it caught me off guard like so many events that year.

It was a hot, rainless, and humid day when the landscapers finally came to plant the trees we'd ordered for the front garden. The tall Japanese maple, the magnolia tree, the dogwood, and the Black Dragon cryptomeria had all been waiting at the nursery. The cryptomeria, an evergreen with a dramatic bend, looked half-dead when it arrived and I feared the others would die before they got a chance to take hold. I learned that day that I take more care with the trees and plants I add to the garden than that landscaping crew did. While it was true that I could never have dug out the large blue spruce, which rested on a gas line, or lifted the heavy trees into place, I certainly would have done a better job of digging a large enough hole, soaking the hole with water, and then adding bone meal or triple mix to give each tree a fighting chance. Rushing at the end of the day, the crew did none of those things.

They plopped the trees in dry holes on the hottest day of the year so far. For weeks after, as the heat wave continued, I had to run a hose on all the trees to keep them from going into shock. When I'd pointed at dry branches falling off the newly planted cryptomeria, the landscape boss said to give it a year, but I could tell within days it wasn't going to make it, so I dug it up and took it back to the nursery. No one cares about a garden as much as the gardener.

In the days before the scheduled CT scan, I fretted over the red maple, which was dropping leaves every day. While I worked to finish the planting in the rearranged front garden, I left the hose running slowing around the maple's roots. The tree had been Peter's pick and I didn't want it to die. Despite the heat and dryness, I added purple day lilies, periwinkle, conical evergreens called Sky Pencil holly, Fothergilla with its bottle-brush flowers, and a cork-screw hazel called *Corylus avellena*, "Red Dragon," to fill out the new beds. I liked the front garden so much more when I was done.

Despite a back that ached from bending, I worked long days, digging, planting, and watering. In the hours of labour, nothing but the garden mattered — not the cancer, not my appearance or age, certainly not the time. I was often out in the garden until we had to leave for medical appointments — including Peter's CT scan — or a Shaw Festival play we'd booked. I knew Peter would be my timekeeper, and sure enough he'd come out and say, "We have to go in half an hour." He never sounded angry or impatient, although I knew he always liked to be early to appointments and events, while I was happy to cut the time as close as I could.

When he called me in, I'd wash just enough to be presentable, and off we'd go with my mind still back in the dirt.

By now, the lilacs were blooming and I couldn't ignore the next stage of the Victory Garden. I planted each small tomato plant against a stake with a slow-releasing spike of fertilizer beside it. I sowed more lettuce, including the Drunken Woman variety that had been my first choice in the winter, and I filled in the remaining rows of root and leafy vegetables. At the back of the garden, the peas were finally pushing up sprouts with tendrils that stretched toward the netting. At the base of each supporting pole, I sowed Armenian cucumber seeds, hoping that despite the loss of my seedlings, I might still get a crop.

When the larger garden bed was completely planted and watered, I stood back, admired it, and tried to imprint in my brain how empty it looked at that moment and how it would change. I knew that growth would come, just as I knew night follows day and day follows night. As the cycles of our daily lives reassure us all, the knowledge that seeds will grow into plants, that tiny tomato seedlings will produce round, delicious fruit, keeps me grounded every year.

While working in the garden continued to bring me some relief during our wait for the results of Peter's scan, it was the trees, always the trees, in our yard that gave Peter some peace. He could sit on our deck for hours staring at the wonderful old canopy at the back of our yard and then go to the front porch to admire the new ones we'd had planted. But he was exhausted from nights of poor sleep and worry. Before his operation in 2012, which had given him his new hip and equal-length legs, his entire body had throbbed with arthritic pain. Except for his back. He'd never had a complaint with his back. It had been a joy to see how much more relaxed his manner had become and how the lines of his face smoothed out when the pain disappeared after his orthopedic surgery. But now, despite the new wedge, he suffered from constant back pain, and I could see the lines tighten again around his eyes. He returned reluctantly to Tylenol, a medication he'd thought he'd said goodbye to.

Even sitting on our deck, where he had usually been able to spend a happy afternoon reading, became painful. The iron chairs surrounding our table dug into a back that had lost fat and muscle mass over the year. I bought two wicker armchairs with thick orange cushions and a cushioned footstool that I thought would be more comfortable for him. They were the best purchase I've ever made. I had Peter back on the deck while I turned my attention to the smaller vegetable garden. When I photographed him smiling in one of the new chairs, he flashed me a *V* for Victory sign.

In the smaller vegetable bed, shoots from my garlic plants stood six inches out of the ground. I tried to imagine what was happening underground. Were the roots stretching farther, the cloves widening to reshape into separate new cloves?

Now that I could see where the garlic plants grew, I planted red-onion seeds in among them. Then, I broke open a cardboard container with dozens of thread-thin roots and planted leeks wherever I could. Next, I moved to the other end of the bed, mounded the dirt into piles, and planted zucchini and butternut squash seedlings into the top of each mound. I'd bought the seedlings from a local nursery after my own had failed. I was too impatient to sow the seeds directly into the soil and wait for them to grow into plants.

About that time, Facebook sent me one of those "your memories from a year ago" reports. It was a photo of a bunch of radishes that I'd posted, and now it was a reminder of how far behind this year's garden was. But I didn't let it get me down. There was nothing usual about this year, and at least now both of my vegetable beds were planted and Peter's surgery was over.

With the sudden heat wave, I had to make an immediate switch from planting to managing garden pests and blights. The heat brought out bugs I didn't usually have to contend with until later in the season. Since one of the principles of my Victory Garden — and my entire garden — was to avoid chemical pesticides, I blasted shrubs and perennials that were invaded by aphids with water. And

I squirted a recipe of canola oil, soap, and water on the black-eyed Susan and Shasta daisy plants that were covered in indeterminable brown spots. When I was watering the tomato plants, I noticed tiny brown spots on their leaves as well. I'd rotated the crops and grown my seedlings from disease-resistant seeds; there shouldn't have been any signs of blight, especially this early in the season. Walking across the yard, I cursed. *Why does it have to be so hard?* Then I stopped and looked around at the beautiful garden beds, at the solid house we owned in the middle of a peaceful region, and I started to laugh at myself. Getting the right combination of water, nutrients, light, and insect control is difficult, yet most plants do thrive and produce. Growing plants is a lot like dealing with cancer: you try to take care of as many factors as you can, but intangibles like the environment and genetics are out of your hands. Yet people, like plants, do survive.

Before our next appointment with Dr. F, Peter searched the internet for connections between back pain and lung cancer, but didn't find any. "I want to know what is going on," he said, "so I can start planning Rome."

I wasn't sure whether Peter felt badly that he'd held us back from our winter trip to India or whether he just wanted another trip to look forward to, but he'd grabbed on to the idea that we should spend November (after putting the garden to bed, of course) in Rome and began searching for flights and an affordable apartment. He kept calling me into his office to point out a great deal on a place that might go fast and I kept cautioning him to wait a few weeks without saying why or fully examining my own caution.

We also talked that month about the wedding we'd always meant to have. Peter and I had officially met in August of 1989 when he came from Halifax to work at the television program *The Journal* on CBC, where I'd been working for a year full-time and

as a freelancer before that. I say "officially" because I had spoken to
him and seen him on a screen a year before meeting him in person.
I had talked to him on the phone about a possible interview with
the host of *The Journal*, Barbara Frum.

Trained as a lawyer at Dalhousie University, Peter was writing
a book about the Donald Marshall inquiry then taking place in
Nova Scotia, an inquiry into how the justice system had impris-
oned a Mi'kmaq man named Donald Marshall for a murder in a
Sydney park that a white man had, in fact, committed. Peter was
also an on-air commentator in Halifax with his friend Parker Barss
Donham, and I was told the two of them were quite an act, so I
booked them both to fill Barbara in on the inquiry when I couldn't
decide which one I thought would be better. My first sighting of
Peter in the edit suite was of a bushy-looking man with a full beard.
I found his manner somewhat ferocious, but I was immediately
impressed with his voice and his forceful, precise speaking manner.

At one point in the interview, Barbara suggested that since
Donald Marshall hadn't spoken articulately at his trial, he hadn't
won the public over to his side, implying perhaps that he was
somewhat at fault for his own conviction. Peter quickly shot back,
"Where's the claim that in order for the justice system to be fair,
impartial, and decent that the individual before them has to be
articulate, well-educated, connected, and rich?"

Apparently, that evening, in the bar in Halifax where Peter
watched the interview with friends, an exclamation of shock filled
the room. Had Peter Kavanagh just dissed the most powerful
media figure in Canada?

If he had, it didn't matter. Once he was working full-time at
The Journal, Barbara became a fan of his, as she was of all sincere,
highly intelligent, highly curious people. "Where did you come
from?" she asked him once when he stunned her with his instant
recall of facts and his persuasive arguments. "Were you trained

by Jesuits?" He'd had Catholic teachers, and some in his family thought he should have become a Jesuit priest. He was a man who stayed in law school because he loved studying the law, even though on his first day in class he knew he never wanted to practise it.

I came back from my holiday that August in 1989 to find Peter sitting at a desk in front of mine. I remember he was wearing a short-sleeved shirt buttoned up to the top, a look that, at first, I thought was kind of geeky. There's an old saying that goes like this: a man falls in love with a woman he's attracted to and a woman becomes attracted to a man she falls in love with. That was certainly true in my case; buttoned-up shirts, beards, and deep voices became more appealing to me the longer I knew Peter. That day, though, he'd made the mistake of having *my* phone book on his desk. Those were the days when chase producers, as we were called because we chased down guests for the daily interviews, lived by our phones, our Rolodexes, and our phone books. And Peter had my phone book, even though "GOODWIN" was written in bold letters on the edge.

"You have my phone book," I said, perhaps a little coldly. He handed it back to me and I set it on my desk, ready for a new season.

Despite that obvious display of my possessiveness, Peter chatted freely to me, as he did with others who surrounded him. He took an interest in everyone and soon found out what they liked to talk about, although that didn't stop him from talking about his own myriad interests. And despite the physical challenges his limp caused him, he made friends with AG, the tall, athletic producer who talked knowingly about basketball, just one of the sports Peter knew nothing about.

We all learned quickly that Peter knew a lot about pretty much everything else, and it wasn't long before producers came to him for help roughing out scripts for late-day paks. Paks were short videos shown before interviews that provided the audience with a background for the story. If a news story broke late or an important interview suddenly came through, then a pak, which had to be researched, written, voiced by the host, and edited for nine o'clock, could be assigned to a producer as late as six. And that was before we had Google or even computers to type scripts on that could be easily revised. We were still using typewriters long after the rest of the world had packed them away.

Peter was about the only person around us who completely understood a clause in Canada's constitution called "the notwithstanding clause" and the only person who could tell you, without looking it up, the ins and outs of the Meech Lake Accord, the accord devised to keep Canada together. As producers came to him to get salient facts so they could quickly get started on their paks, AG jokingly suggested a new segment for the show: "Just Ask Peter."

I liked Peter, but I was far from interested in any relationship at that point. Less than a year earlier, I'd discovered my husband of more than a decade was having an affair and wanted out of our marriage. I was determined to work through my sense of betrayal and abandonment and to figure out a way for me and Jane, who was then a toddler, to live well, since they say living well is the best revenge. I was seeing counsellors and reading relevant books, determined to pick myself up. My mother always liked to tell us to "get back up on the horse again." I never rode horses, was a bit afraid of them, but I understood her meaning. My ex was not going to keep me down.

Still, I found myself more and more intrigued by Peter and surprised to find myself wondering what connection I had to this man. It was at a birthday party for me that fall at a friend's house that Peter, perhaps after a beer or two or three, came up to me and said, "I like you."

I ignored the noise of the party around me and answered, "I like you, too," while looking around the room, but not at him. I could still see him shake his head, though.

"No. I really like you," he said. "Can we go for a coffee after?"

It was well past the hour when I drink coffee, but Jane was away that weekend with her father at his parents' home, so I had no reason to go home. And I was curious enough to agree.

I drove us east from my friend's house and we looked for a coffee shop that was open. We finally ended up at a Coffee Time on Queen Street East near my home, a place I'd never thought to go to when I passed it on the streetcar on my way to work.

We spent much of the night drinking coffee there. Later, I'd hear Peter say again and again, "I can fall asleep drinking coffee." But caffeine in the late night had me buzzing and alert. Even though we avoided drinking their coffee forever after, we had Coffee Time mugs for years to remember that night. Well into the morning hours we talked about ourselves, two wounded souls who wanted more in life.

Peter talked about a year of separation from his family after he contracted polio as a two-month-old infant, about the experiments done on him as a child to lengthen his semi-paralyzed left leg, about the year he spent in a body cast when his leg was fused to his pelvis with a silver plate because doctors had missed the fact he'd had a dislocated hip at birth, so that by the time Peter was twelve he had worn out the socket and the ball of his left hip.

As cab drivers stepped in for coffees to keep them awake and drifters came and went, I talked about believing my marriage had been good, about how my husband and I had been best friends, how my daughter and dream job had finally come into my life after years of waiting for both, and how I thought I'd been owed some time to enjoy my daughter and the job after putting my husband through graduate school. It was as though we were setting our cards on the table. Those were the hands we'd been dealt, but neither of us wanted them to be who we were or where we were going.

After that night, there was never any talk about dating others, or of not being together. However, I was slow to trust in a second chance at love. The first time we went out to dinner together, we walked from his apartment in downtown Toronto to a nearby restaurant called Le Paradis.

"Well, with a name like that they're setting us up for rather high expectations," I said, with bitter cynicism in my voice.

"There's nothing wrong with high expectations," Peter said.

I have always remembered that moment when my cynicism slipped a little. I think I came to see how optimism had kept Peter going, and I think I started to fall in love with him a moment later.

Still, I didn't want to rush Jane into any new living arrangement and wanted to do all I could to spend more time with her. That fall, I left *The Journal* for a job with CBC Newsworld after a senior producer from the new cable channel phoned *The Journal* and I answered.

"Are you happy there?" she asked.

I *was* happy there. Being at *The Journal*, surrounded by all those smart, funny people, was my ideal job. But at *The Journal* I often didn't know if I'd have to work through the evenings, and I didn't like the idea of handing Jane over to a babysitter without any preparation or of negotiating with my ex on the fly about child care.

The woman explained she needed a producer to help her with weekend programming for the new network.

"Can I go home at five?"

"Yes," she answered.

It was enough for me. I loved the idea of being able to spend my evenings with Jane. But the work at Newsworld was a disappointment after the excitement at *The Journal*. I basically had to figure out ways to fill hours of airtime with no money.

When the possibility of moving to Ottawa to create a program for the network came up at the same time as my ex's request that we sell our house and divide the profits, I jumped at the job. My ex had suggested I could move somewhere cheaper than the Beaches, the Toronto neighbourhood where we lived, somewhere out of the city on the highway like Ajax (ignoring my dislike of suburbs or perhaps throwing it in my face). So Ottawa, where I could afford a house in a downtown neighbourhood, seemed like a good fit.

I had been reading that a drop in economic status after a separation contributed to the negative effects on children. And I believed that was one aspect of Jane's situation I could control. With my share of the Toronto house, I bought a good, older house in Ottawa. The previous owners had left a swing set in the back-yard, which Jane ran to the moment she saw it, releasing some of her anxiety about the move to a new home. The yard offered me enough space for a decent-sized vegetable garden, which gave me an equal amount of comfort. Once the two of us were settled there, we strolled winter weekends on nearby Bank Street, where we stopped at a small Italian shop for hot chocolate, walked along the canal on wet spring evenings so Jane could jump in the pud-dles, and carried summer picnics to a nearby pond.

Moving to Ottawa also meant I could get away from my mother. In Toronto, she'd taken to phoning me and urging me to do all I could to get my husband back at a time when I was trying to accept that my marriage had ended. When I'd first broken the news of my collapsing marriage, my parents had come to my house with baskets of flowers, fruits, and vegetables. I'd felt loved and was grateful that they could be there for me in a way I needed. But it hadn't taken long for my mother to begin nagging, telling me that I had prob-ably let myself go after having Jane, seeming to put all the blame on me. The counsellor I was seeing advised me to tell my mother I was going to hang up the phone whenever she started in on me.

It took me a while, but soon I was able to repeatedly say, "I'm going to hang up now. I'm going to hang up now."

Even then, I recognized my mother was scared for me and Jane, as well as a bit ashamed about having a daughter who couldn't keep her husband. Don't get me wrong; my mother was a generous woman who endorsed and financed, along with my father, all her children's choices for university, including my year abroad. She had won top honours in university herself and considered a career as a lawyer before switching to becoming a teacher. But she'd bought in to postwar domesticity, and impressed on her daughters the need for husbands. I just couldn't deal with her contradictions and fears. I needed a time out from her. In later years, our relationship mellowed to a point where I enjoyed driving her around the Niagara Region, listening to stories of her childhood and the goldenrod and blue asters that grew in ditches then.

I wasn't trying to keep Peter out of my life by moving, but I knew that could be a consequence of living in a different city. But all he said was "There's a train to Ottawa and I'll be on it."

And I planned to go to Toronto frequently on weekends for Jane's visits with her father. Peter and I were both determined to make it work. He was good to his word about coming weekends on the train, and our passion and comfort with each other blossomed on our frequent visits over the three years we were apart.

It was Jane who finally said to Peter one day on the phone, "Why don't you live with us?" Soon after, I sold my house in Ottawa and we all moved into a home in the west end of Toronto. I went back to a job like my old one at CBC, where I was able to begin travelling to produce documentaries.

So, although we had loved each other for twenty-seven years and had lived together for twenty-three, we had never made our union official. For years, I was afraid to mess with the separation agreement I had with Jane's father; divorce proceedings had the potential of opening the whole arrangement again. Later, life, work, holidays, and health issues all seemed to take priority, even after my divorce became final when Jane was in university.

There was even a time, when Peter was smoking cigarettes, that I told him I'd always be there for him but I could not say the words *in sickness and health* while he was smoking. He saw that as a threat, I think, and I suppose it was. He didn't respond well to threats and he gave up smoking in his own time, but we never got around to the wedding. The first full summer in our new house in Niagara-on-the-Lake, we'd talked about a ceremony again, but left the planning too late. We decided now, that if we sent out invitations in June, we could have a wedding in our garden in August, the month we'd met.

On the night before Peter's appointment for his CT scan, we went to Wednesday supper in Niagara-on-the-Lake, a summer tradition; local wineries and food trucks gather in a green space near our home and people from both the town and the region come and sit outdoors at picnic tables painted in pastel colours or on lawn chairs to eat fresh food and listen to live music. Because Peter had to call me in from the garden, we arrived late and the people with the truck that pulled a wood-burning oven were sold out of our favourite margherita pizzas. Instead, we split a lamb burger barbecued by a local butcher and each got a glass of wine. As we sat in the folding chairs we'd bought just for Wednesday suppers, I raised the topic of our wedding to give us something hopeful to talk about. We'd keep the guest list small, the food as local as possible, with offerings from the garden, put a tent on the lawn in case of rain. But we ended up returning to the subject we'd been avoiding: the next day and the few words that could send our lives in different directions, either to travel and a wedding or to cancer treatments again. A clean scan or one spotted with cancer.

We waited longer than usual for our appointment with Dr. F the next day. Our breathing became faster, our sighs louder as we sat in the waiting area. Neither of us spoke. When a resident finally called us into an examining room, he wanted to look at Peter's incision first and was surprised to find it still red and leaking. He said Dr. F would "discuss the plan" and left the room, left us not knowing if the plan to be discussed was for the incision that wouldn't heal or the return of cancer. His avoidance of the topic of cancer left me on edge, but I tried not to imagine the worst. It was something Peter often accused me of doing and cautioned me against. "Don't get ahead of the narrative," he'd say.

When Dr. F finally came into the room, he too began by examining Peter's incision and talking about why it was taking so long to heal. My stomach knotted as Dr. F described how some dissolving stitches were still stuck in two places, preventing the spots from closing. He asked me if I wanted to leave the room while he pulled the stitches out, but I wasn't going anywhere. My stomach knotted further as he dug into the incision and Peter grunted with the pain. I was sure Peter was having the same thoughts I was: *Why isn't he mentioning the scan?* But with Peter stretched out on the examining bed and enduring pokes with a pair of tweezers, I decided it was up to me to ask about the scan. Before I could, though, Dr. F mentioned — almost as an aside — that he'd want another scan in three months because he still had concerns over the scar tissue that had made the surgery so difficult.

"But there's no cancer on this scan?" I asked.

"No," he said as though we already knew that, and perhaps he thought the resident had given us that information. But as a storyteller, a journalist, someone who had been waiting for that word, I wanted to scream, *Talk about burying the lead!*

Then, as he helped Peter sit up, Dr. F listened to Peter's concerns about his back pain. "It isn't cancer," the doctor said. "It sounds muscular-skeletal. It might have to do with weight loss and changed sleeping habits," he admitted. It was clear, though, that if it wasn't cancer and it wasn't a surgical issue, it was outside his realm. Still, the weight-loss theory matched the opinions of Peter's physiotherapist and a top-notch masseuse we saw when we could. They had both recommended back-strengthening exercises and Peter was working on those at the gym.

Driving home, we didn't feel the joy we'd hoped would come with the words *no cancer*. There was something about the way Dr. F qualified the results, the caution about the scar tissue, that dampened our mood. Still, we had the outcome we'd been waiting for since that long day in the surgical wing. No cancer. It was enough for Peter to decide to get on with things, to keep searching for his new normal, enough for me to hope we'd have more years of travel, writing, and spending time in the garden. When I got home, I added the weekend in Casablanca to my itinerary. Together, we worked on the wording for our wedding invitation, and at his desk, Peter surfed for apartments in Rome.

A true gardener, especially a Victory Gardener, would never leave the field in the middle of the battle, but I did my best to prepare the beds for ten days without me. I pulled up the small but delicious radishes, weeded the rows, thinned the beets and carrots, sprayed other plants with my natural insecticide concoction, and showed Peter how to use the various hoses that circled our garden.

Before I left, we had birthdays to celebrate. For Peter's sixty-third birthday on June 12, he and I drove to the nearby village of Jordan and had lunch in a favourite inn that overlooked the deep valley, now green with summer. The restaurant had a take on fish and chips with local perch that appealed to Peter. He ate all his fish and, with my enthusiastic help, all his fries, and we even ordered a dessert to share.

Back home, Peter posted two pictures from our lunch on Facebook: one of our lemon chiffon dessert with fruit and cream before we'd demolished it, and one of an empty plate along with these words: "The new normal birthday edition. I alone could not eat this, but with the assistance of the dearest person alive, Debi Goodwin, the dessert was done and it was delicious."

Two days later, on the fourteenth, we drove to Toronto to celebrate Jane's thirtieth birthday with family at an upscale Italian restaurant. There, Peter managed to eat a main course of lamb and had enough energy to enjoy the evening. When I left for my trip days after that, I felt okay about going. *We are on our way*, I thought. *Peter is recovering.*

Chapter Eleven

IT WAS ONLY DURING MY TRIP to Spain that my body and mind recognized how slammed they'd been by the past seven months. The effect started the day I left. I spent so much time getting the garden in shape that I ended up leaving Niagara-on-the-Lake later than planned and worried my way through heavy traffic. Cursing myself. Feeling like a fool. At Terminal 3, which I seldom used, I found the automated check-in rushed and confusing. As I lined up to put my suitcase through an X-ray machine, an airline representative came up to me with my passport. I had left it in the machine reader. I suddenly felt old, incompetent, and, although I had always been a traveller and an expert at getting through airports and keeping my belongings safe, a travel newbie. In the wide space beside the gates, there were rows and rows of tables where relaxed people ordered food from iPads. I sat at a table and drank from a bottle of water I'd bought and felt like weeping. It had been a rough winter and this was the first time I'd sat down without anything needing to be done or without anything to distract me. There were no weeds to pull, no insects to blast off plants.

The press trip itself was delightful. S, from the Spanish consulate in Toronto, had organized an intensive itinerary through

Andalusia. Each day was jam-packed, with little time left for anything but sleep and a quick nightly look at my photographs and notes of the day's excursions. We were wined and dined on all the best the region had to offer; shepherded through a tourist-filled Alhambra and sleepy medieval towns in blistering summer weather. The group was small, just five Canadian writers travelling with S and a local guide. A friendly group, but I kept to myself a lot, lost in thought about Peter, still worried despite the last scan.

One day my ankles swelled up and that night I woke up with chest pains. I was convinced, after an internet search, that I had congestive heart failure and someone would find me dead in my bed. I had managed to keep such irrational fears at bay when I was taking care of Peter, getting him to appointments and trying to boost his spirits. Alone, my fear demons took over. In the morning, I discovered my ankles had been swollen from the straps on my sandals that had been pulled too tight and my chest pains were the first sign of a cold. I would most certainly live.

At the end of the six days I wished I was going back home with the others. I was sick and woke up to learn that Great Britain had voted to leave the European Union, unsettling news in trying times. I wanted to get back to my touchstones: Peter and my garden. But I continued to my weekend in Casablanca, which unfortunately involved an extra day to make the right flight connections.

The city was in the middle of Ramadan and many of the restaurants were shut for the month, the Grand Mosque closed to non-Muslims. Still, with my friend as my guide, I enjoyed walking the city and bargaining at the local souk where the shopkeepers were, to my delight, easygoing, perhaps out of exhaustion. During the long nights, a steady flow of cars sped below the open windows of my friend's apartment. As I imagined those occupants revelling between their two meals of Ramadan, I felt a deep homesickness that I hadn't experienced since I'd gone to France on my own as a twenty-year-old student, a wrenching fear that I would have years ahead of feeling alone and disoriented.

Over the ten days I was away, Peter and I communicated through email. In our efforts to be kind to each other, I suspect, he played down his pain and, I discovered only later, his new problems with eating, and I downplayed the gourmet food I was sampling and the amazing sites of Moorish culture in Spain that he was missing. Peter wrote of thirty-degree days and no rain and reassured me he was watering. He wrote of good sleeps and bad sleeps, walks to the post office, a successful speech in support of the local library, and eating the first ripe patio tomato. Our neighbour had driven Peter to Hamilton one day for an appointment with Dr. F, and Peter wrote that the incision was finally healing and Dr. F was pleased with his progress. At that meeting, Peter noticed Dr. F seemed down and asked him how he was doing. I suspect Dr. F was unused to patients inquiring after him. Dr. F told Peter that there were days when he had to tell too many patients there wasn't anything he could do for them, and that day had been one of them.

When I got home the whole region looked parched. We were in the midst of the longest drought in thirty years. The lawn at the community centre was completely brown. Around town, it was easy to tell which owners watered; their green lawns stood out like small oases in a desert. Our lawn was somewhere in between the extremes, but we decided to water to make sure it looked fresh for our wedding. There was no water ban in our area, but our bill would be high.

Peter had done his best to keep my garden alive while I was away. There was lettuce to eat and plenty of Swiss chard. There'd be daily meals with both for the rest of the month, with enough to spare for neighbours and visitors. There were some peas to pick, too. And soon there'd be a summer's supply of beans, carrots, and beets. To my relief, the tomato plants appeared to be in good condition, with healthy green leaves and small green fruit. But the rapini I'd planted more than a month earlier had already bolted into bitterness and was now a total loss. Before leaving, I had set my small cabbage plants, grown first in pots on the deck, into the bed, and I could see now that only a few of them would make it to full-sized cabbages. Most surprising was the zucchini, a variety that had been so prolific the year before but was definitely underperforming now.

Next to the zucchini and butternut squash vines, the garlic stems were tall and thick, curling into scapes. If I didn't cut the scapes, they would open as flowers, draining the plants' energy, which I wanted directed into fattening up the cloves underground. I had first learned how to grow garlic and when to cut the scapes from a hairdresser in Toronto, a Vietnamese Canadian who kept his traditional cuisine vibrant with garlic grown in his suburban garden. It was only after Peter and I visited Vietnam that I fully realized how important fresh herbs were to the cuisine, especially to the traditional pho, and I wondered what else D had grown in his garden: hot peppers, cilantro, basil, maybe even lemon grass, which I now had growing in my own herb garden. Even though D warned me to cut the scapes, I sometimes didn't get to them in time during busy work years. I was rewarded with big round white flower heads so beautiful my neighbour decided to plant garlic in her front flower bed. But during those years of negligence, the garlic cloves I pulled up at the end of summer were small and had little taste. When I finally became more diligent about cutting the scapes at the right time, I stored them in plastic bags in the refrigerator. Lots of recipes call for scapes to add a slight garlic taste to food, but I never found one I liked. Most years, they sit in my fridge for weeks until I finally throw them into a broth.

With the first inspection of the garden finished, I caught up with Peter on the deck. He admitted then that his digestive system was giving him trouble, and as we ate, I could see he was eating less than before I'd left for my trip.

"It's not like before, though," he said to reassure me. "There's no problem with my swallowing." He added that there were just days now when his new, reduced stomach couldn't handle the food he ate.

As someone who had spent too much time in hospital beds as a child, prodded by nurses and doctors, Peter never liked to talk about the inner workings of his body. Part of becoming an adult was being able to keep that all to himself. But now he talked to me about his digestive system in a way he never would have before. We booked an appointment with our family doctor to find ways to deal with his new problems and we finally bought a good digital scale to keep an accurate record of his weight at home. On the last day of June, we discovered he was down to 162 pounds, from the 187 he'd been in April. With the desserts and wines of Spain, I'd gained weight and I was not far behind him.

Peter had been reading as much as he could about digestion and weight loss after esophageal cancer surgery, and nothing he was experiencing was beyond the limits of the normal body response. On one site he visited online, a Harvard doctor's site, the doctor reported that when a man who had gone through the same surgery as Peter complained of digestive problems, he told him that it had only been a year; it was early days.

Despite the setbacks, on the July long weekend we drove to visit A and D in New York State. We had met them on a train trip in India eleven years earlier and had been exchanging visits ever since. We drove that weekend to their second home, a house on top of a mountain road that overlooked the Adirondacks one way and the Catskills the other. A had been adding fruit trees to the property over the years: apples, plums, and peaches. She and her husband, a man who gently blamed me for A's increasing desire to garden, had dug through heavy shale to create holes big enough for each tree. Despite the conditions, many of the trees had already given them fruit.

Russian Jews by origin, A and D were hosting other Russians that weekend, and Peter was in full form, entertaining them with his stories and jokes, his booming voice as strong as ever. Perhaps only I noticed how little food he put on his plate.

While we'd lived in Toronto, our friends' country home in New York had always been a welcome escape from the city; they had given us a key and told us to visit whenever we wanted. Each summer we drove to a pick-your-own farm with them to harvest cherries, berries, and vegetables, and this time we found black raspberries. Ever since the naturopath had told us that black raspberries were effective in reducing esophageal tumours, I'd kept up my hunt for them. When I told A, a radiologist, about the clinical studies I'd read, she helped me fill baskets with the berries.

Even so, I felt eager to get back to my own garden and to get on with finding out why eating had grown more difficult for Peter. I measured my own concerns about Peter's eating against A's and again felt somewhat reassured. A was a doctor, after all. She suggested a specific probiotic to improve Peter's digestion. I stocked up on it before we left the States in case it wasn't available in Canada.

After we got home from our short outing, my first battle in the garden was with Japanese beetles, which were already nibbling on my roses, my cherry trees, and the furry leaves of my Kentucky Wonder beans. I'd first encountered Japanese beetles the previous summer. When I'd come out one morning, I discovered roses filled with holes and metallic blue-green beetles hiding beneath the flower petals. I'd begun to read about the beetles and search for the best ways to eradicate them. There was no way to eradicate them.

It's suspected that *Popillia japonica* arrived in New Jersey in 1915 as grubs in soil around the roots of irises imported from Japan. A year later the beetles emerged and began their destruction and their spread across the eastern United States. With no natural enemies in their new home, they encountered no resistance. One scientist reported that in 1923 he filled thirteen barrels with beetles shaken from the peach trees of one orchard, only to discover the trees covered again the next morning.

Even if I had been open to the idea of chemical pesticides, there were none that would kill just the beetle. Frustrated famers in the past turned to poisons that wiped out all insects in their path, including helpful bees. I was never going to use such draconian methods. I would never do anything to contribute to the depletion of the bees that are so important to our environment. And I certainly wasn't going to travel to the States to buy harsh pesticides that were now restricted in Ontario.

In an over-the-fence chat with a neighbour at the back of our yard the first summer in our new neighbourhood, I'd complained about the damage the beetles were doing to my roses. He'd shrugged philosophically and said he simply cut all his flowers from the bushes once the beetles started to appear, which had made me wonder why he had roses at all. He'd told me there were traps I could buy, traps a former neighbour had frequently used that had helped the whole block. I'd already read that the traps were a bad idea, that the pheromones inside them attracted so many beetles, they quickly filled up and the gardener was left with even more beetles flying around. I'd told him that. With another shrug of his shoulders, he'd let the matter drop. And I became determined to not buy the traps and become the bull's eye for beetles in the neighbourhood. Besides, in my reading, I had discovered what I thought would be my weapons of choice in this battle: a Mason jar filled with soapy warm water and a paintbrush.

Throughout the winter, when I had thought of cancer cells, I'd envisioned Japanese beetles as the bad cells eating away at the good cells of the beautiful roses. So, when I discovered I had a second year of the unwelcome invasion, I went out in the early mornings and swiped the unsuspecting beetles into a jar of warm soapy water and then swirled the water around with the paintbrush so they couldn't get out before they drowned. I must admit I took pleasure in watching their little legs stop twitching and in counting how many beetles I'd trapped at the end of each day. At least I was able to take action against one harmful invader.

I'd done enough research to add a preventive measure in my second year of war against the Japanese beetle. Neem oil, non-toxic oil that comes from the seeds of the neem tree, native to South Asia, has long been shown to repel insects. Better still, it does no harm to bees as long as they are not on the plant when it is being sprayed. Neem oil is not registered as a pesticide in Canada and therefore isn't sold in garden centres. However, I could find only small risks to using the product; it could damage plants if it was sprayed too heavily, too frequently, and in the heat of the day, all things I could control and monitor. Ironically, organic neem oil was considered safe enough to be sold freely in Canada for the skin and for medicinal purposes. But the small bottles available online were an expensive way to purchase it for garden use.

I found my neem oil at a local rose centre, known all over the continent for its wide selection of rose varieties. The nursery was owned by a couple who had emigrated from Switzerland. The husband especially was incredibly knowledgeable about all things horticultural and had no qualms about selling neem oil as a pesticide. I sprayed my neem oil on the roses in the early hours; the plants remained unharmed and the number of visits by Japanese beetles did decrease. I was more sparing with the spray on my beans, uncertain if the bitter oil applied to the leaves would affect the taste of my crop. Well into August, I had to visit the beans each day with my soapy water and paintbrush.

Throughout July, Peter had moments when his old irritability surfaced. In the past few peaceful years, I'd almost forgotten about the irritability that had accompanied his chronic pain before his body was surgically made even. Then I remembered how, more than two decades earlier, when we'd all become a household together, Jane and I would independently come into the kitchen and, in response to a grimace on Peter's face, ask, "Are you mad at me?"

It took us months to realize the morning grimaces had nothing to do with us, and we both learned to let moments of crossness slide, to save any important questions for later when Peter's pain was better under control. This time around, I immediately recognized the grimaces as a symptom of his new pain and viewed them with alarm.

Still, Peter wanted to keep on planning our wedding. We visited an Italian caterer in St. Catharines to order appetizers. We stocked up on wine and Prosecco, bought extra cutlery at Ikea. Peter took on the task of finding someone who would marry us. Neither of us wanted a religious ceremony, and through our real-estate lawyer in town, Peter found a service called Dream Weddings. Despite the fantasy name, it seemed like a good fit. An officiant who could legally marry couples would oversee whatever ceremony we wanted.

In the middle of July, the officiant, J, asked to meet us to go over our plans for the wedding. We agreed to a time one Friday afternoon in Burlington so we could pick Jane up at the GO Train station there and bring her home for the weekend. As we talked in a coffee shop, J soon realized we didn't want "the dream wedding," and offered us the cheapest package. But as we kept scratching out lines from his script, he seemed a little alarmed that there wouldn't be much for him to do.

We tried to tell him we were both writers, both producers, and we would write our own vows. And that was all we wanted. Even so, he didn't seem to get how minimalist we wanted the ceremony to be. He asked who would give me away.

"No one is giving me away," I answered. *Why would any sixty-five-year-old woman want to be given away?*

"What prayers would you like me to read?"

I looked at Peter, who was sitting back, letting me answer the questions. "We don't want any prayers."

"Will there be music?"

"No," we both said. We didn't want to bring speakers out into the quiet of our backyard.

"Will the dress be formal or informal?"

"Informal," I said.

He must have sensed I was growing frustrated with his questions. "I just need to know whether I should wear a jacket and tie or can come in a summer shirt," he said.

I nodded, hoping the questions were over.

He looked at the page before him with so many sections scratched out. "And Peter," he said, perhaps hoping for more conciliation from the man at my side. "You'll say your vows first."

We both must have looked at him quizzically. "It's the bride's day," J said. I cringed at the old thinking, but also wondered why, if it was the bride's day, she didn't get to go first. But I didn't say anything; Peter and I could make that decision later. I wanted this process over. As a girl, I'd always despised the roles assigned to women in bible stories and the expectations of them in my family, especially of brides at weddings.

Even when I'd first married at twenty-three, I hadn't wanted a big wedding. But after I'd suggested a very small ceremony to my mother, she'd burst into the bathroom where I lay naked in the bath and accused me of being either pregnant or ashamed of my fiancé. To her, those were the only reasons a young woman in the 1970s might not want all the hoopla, the only reasons I would deny her the opportunity to invite all her friends and relatives to a good show. I was her last child but her first chance to put on a big wedding. Faced with her hysteria, I'd told her coldly to do what she wanted and I'd be there. And my wedding day had ended up being more about her wishes than mine. I wasn't about to let anything like that happen again.

Finally, J seemed to get it. The simplest of ceremonies. I thought we were all set, but then he began to ask questions. "To get to know you better," he said.

"Why?" I asked with suspicion.

"So I can introduce you."

I have never been very good at confrontation. Over the years I've learned to speak up when I must, but I've never learned the right tone to use. I tried this time. "This isn't personal," I said. "But I don't see someone who doesn't know us introducing us to people who have known us, I'd say, on average for about twenty-five years."

It was Peter who saved the moment. He sat quietly listening to my objections, watching J's discomfort. "I might have a solution," he said. He turned to J. "How about I write something that you could say to start the ceremony and send it to you?"

J welcomed that solution, appeared relieved the matter was settled. And we all left the meeting intact. As Peter and I drove to pick up Jane, I felt lighter. And I was reminded how much I loved Peter, not just for his wisdom and compassion, but for the way he let me be who I was. The only times Peter pushed me was when he thought I was being too self-effacing.

After returning from my travels straight to dealing with drought and concerns about keeping the wedding and Peter's eating on track, I felt out of rhythm with the garden. Weather reports teased us with promises of rain, but there'd been none in the past week and little all month. The promised thunderstorms all seemed to roll over us and drop their rain on nearby locations. It seemed to me I spent most of my time keeping the garden from drying out. I left the hose dribbling on the new trees, watered the vegetables, and moved the sprinkler from yellow spot to yellow spot on the lawn. A drought is not the best time to feed plants, since they are doing all they can just to survive, but I still tried to give them some nutritional support. My zucchini plants were having the hardest time. Baby-finger-sized fruit would appear, stay that size for a week or so, and then finally shrivel up. My crop was reduced to a few fruits that somehow survived hidden under leaves. I would certainly not be able to feed any nation, no matter how small.

I deadheaded any wilted roses, partly to thwart the Japanese beetles and partly to give the plants a rest so they would bloom again once the weather grew cooler. When I'd been walking with A around her flower garden in New York, she'd praised the benefits of Epsom salts turned into the soil around the roots of her roses. But in searching the internet, I found mixed reviews, even one from a reputable horticultural site that said the salt could harm the plants. Most sites said Epsom salts help grow bigger tomatoes, peppers, and roses if the soil lacks magnesium; others said magnesium deficiencies are not that common and not to add it without testing the soil. As an experiment, I added some Epsom salts to a couple of roses and realized again that keeping plants healthy was a bit like trying to solve Peter's eating problems. Despite all the medical science that exists, everything still felt like trial and error. Probiotics: yes, no, maybe. And food that appeared as good choices on one list appeared on others as bad. I wanted clear answers, obvious solutions, but once again had to accept the middle ground of confused attempts to get things right.

Three weeks before the wedding, Peter weighed 161 pounds. Our family doctor sent him to a dietitian, who came up with a long list of digestible, high-calorie, nutritious foods for him to stick to and a strict schedule of eating small meals every two hours during the day. When he had been trying to keep his weight up in the fall during his cancer treatments, he had drunk cans of chocolate Ensure or Boost for the calories but he'd hated the chemical aftertaste. The dietitian told us of a juice form of the drink that was more palatable but hard to find. On the way home, we ordered a case of it from our local drugstore. The visits to the doctor and the dietitian accomplished two things: they reassured us that both the digestive problems were understandable after the drastic rearrangement of his system that Peter had gone through and that there were things we could do to keep him from losing more weight. And later, on our second visit to the dietitian, she seemed pleased that Peter's weight loss was levelling off and came up with more strategies to get his digestive system working more consistently.

Food once again became a battleground instead of a pleasure. The folding chairs we'd used most weeks the previous summer for Wednesday suppers remained hanging on the garage wall, and once again we avoided eating out or dining with others. At home, Peter would start to eat a favourite food and not be able to finish it, or he'd suggest something he wanted to eat for supper and then not want to bother with it because he felt too bloated. More and more he relied on the supplemental juice drink.

The midsummer bountifulness of the garden seemed pointless. In fact, it felt like an affront because Peter showed no interest in any of it. I harvested peas, chard, lettuce, beans, and beets and wondered why I'd grown all these vegetables. The difference in our dinner plates that summer was stark. Peter's plate, with its small slice of baked chicken pot pie, looked spartan, while my plate, supplemented with yellow beets, red-stemmed Swiss chard, and zucchini stir-fried with tomatoes and onions, was a riot of colours and nutrients.

In gardens, as in life, you just keep doing what you think you need to do. I didn't want the garden to grow rampant. It felt especially important that July to get at least one thing under control, to not let the garden slide into a midsummer funk along with my spirits. Near the end of the month, I had T over for the afternoon for jobs that required more strength than I had. While we worked, I told T that Peter and I were getting married in the garden and I needed everything to look its best. He seemed surprised we weren't already married, so I gave him the one-minute summary: I hadn't got a divorce until a few years back. But it was enough of a statement to open the door to a long story of his relationship with his new girlfriend. B was Catholic, a married Catholic wanting a divorce from an ex who resisted giving her one even though he didn't want to be with her.

When five rolled around, I wanted to stop, but T said he'd like to get some dinner and then work into the evening. In the past, I might have offered him something to eat, but I didn't feel like doing that when meals were so troublesome in our house. Instead, I asked if he'd go to a local pub he favoured. That question opened the door to another story about how the pub's recent renovations had ruined the place. In the past he'd been able to get a large plate of fries there for five dollars; now the fries had sea salt and came as a small side. On top of that, the owners had taken out the pool table to add more seating. He had met B at that pool table. But he knew where to get the best bargains in town; he'd go to the local grocery store where they sold hot potato wedges. I didn't have the energy to question him about his devotion to healthy food.

He'd had plans, T told me, perhaps a bit defensively, to go climbing with some buddies but they were all off playing Pokémon. He seemed annoyed and bewildered by their decision to suddenly choose that old game over an evening with him. It became apparent to me he hadn't heard of the *Pokémon Go* app, which had become an international craze that summer. I tried to explain it to him as best I could.

"That sounds kind of fun," he said, unembarrassed that an older woman was telling him about a young man's game.

The waning days of July were stinking hot, with no rain. In between garden tasks and medical appointments, I helped pack up an apartment without air conditioning that had sat empty for six months, waiting for the Syrian family our local committee had attempted to sponsor. We had rented the apartment in February when we'd received word that our family would arrive shortly; members of our committee had lovingly furnished and stocked it while I'd been by Peter's side after his surgery. But by midsummer our family was still stuck in Turkey and the Canadian government's effort to clear refugees like ours had lost momentum. It was another disappointment in a disappointing summer. I had taken on the task of being one of the people who communicated with the family's father through Google translation, but I was running out of ways to reassure him, especially since I was so focused on figuring out ways to keep myself calm.

Then, on the last night of July, it rained. It poured. I woke to the sound of thunder and the electric thrill of negative ions in the air. In the early morning, I remembered the orange cushions were still on the chairs on the deck; it had been so long since I'd had to worry about them getting wet. I ran downstairs and out into the warm rain. It was six-thirty and the solar lamps in the garden were shutting off one by one. But as rain clouds passed overhead, they darkened the skies and confused the lights' sensors. Was it day? Was it night? The lamps began blinking off and on.

I stood for a while watching the lights as their sensors tried to read the skies. I didn't mind standing in the rain; it washed away the knots of depression that had been gathering in my stomach, muscles, and mind. I felt excited by the rain, excited by the possibility that not everything always went downhill, that good news — like a good rain — could surprise you. The garden would green up on its own. And no one had given us any suggestion that Peter couldn't get better. The solar lamps continued to twinkle, caught between light and darkness, a place I understood all too well.

Chapter Twelve

IT WAS THE BEST OF MONTHS; it was the worst of months. A riff on Dickens that ran through my head like a bad radio song as summer days grew cooler. It's a poor writer who relies on the words of others. But if I'm being kind to myself — and I feel I must be — it could simply be that a patterned phrase rescued me from a gut-wrenching search for my own words. Like the gardener who buys hanging baskets of petunias and pots of patio tomatoes, I just didn't have the energy or the desire to get down on my knees in the dirt. To dig past the pain and shock. The extreme between the high and the low of the month was just too cruel to absorb.

August began with a push in the garden. Even though rain had finally arrived, I still had to water the beds and the grass in the days that followed to keep everything at its best. I wanted the garden perfect for August sixth, the day Peter and I would get married. I was obsessive about it, worked for hours each day to pull weeds, deadhead perennials, and keep the Japanese beetle at bay. As if by making the garden perfect, the day perfect, I could make everything all right.

Peter's pain and eating problems persisted. When he wasn't having stomach cramps, he was groaning from back pain. I'd suggested in late July that we postpone the wedding until we sorted out his postsurgery issues.

"I'll be fine when the day comes," he said. "That day will be the highlight of my life."

I was touched by his choice of words but also a little frightened by them. But since he was not in a mood to postpone anything, I continued taking care of the details for our wedding.

Only there was nothing fine about his state of health as the day approached. At night, he'd lie on his side in his white undershirt and ask, "Would you rub my back?" I would stretch out a hand from my side of the bed and gently stroke his back through the shirt. There was none of the playfulness we used to have at bedtime: Me making up silly songs and him singing the love song he'd created. "*I'm in love with a beautiful woman,*" he'd intone. "*She's from Grimsby, Ontario. She grows green beans, dill, and tomatoes. And rides her scooter on the escarpment solo.*" For years, he'd been playing with a second verse but he'd given up on that. I hadn't heard the first one in months. Still, we had to believe that despite the back pain and the eating problems, everyone — the doctors, the dietitian, the physiotherapist — was right when they told us Peter's symptoms all fit with a rocky recovery. I had to believe we'd already had our victory on the cancer front and Peter would beat these postsurgical difficulties, too.

Outside, my Victory Garden had suffered as I turned my attention to the other gardens before the wedding. In the early days of August, I went back to it. I tried to get the tomatoes under control with more stakes and ties. Ironically, I had no problem with my indeterminate tomatoes, the Big Beef, which grew tall and straight. While I had pulled suckers from them to keep them from getting rangy, I hadn't needed to do it often, even if they now leaned a bit under the weight of fat tomatoes. It was the Romas, the variety described as determinate tomatoes, which were supposed to stay bushy and controlled, that sprawled everywhere, with some weak stems falling to the ground. In July, I'd pushed more stakes into the soil around their perimeter and wrapped twine around the stakes to hold the drooping plants. And, while I'd picked some tomatoes to eat from the various plants around the yard and on the deck, the bulk of my tomatoes were smaller than they should have been by early August and they were still very green. The platters of sliced homegrown tomatoes with basil I'd pictured on the wedding buffet table were not to be.

There were bare patches in the Victory Garden, too, where I'd pulled out lettuce that had bolted. I'd tried to fill the gaps with other crops, but in the heat wave the seeds had refused to sprout. So I left one row of bitter lettuce for its colour — like the inside of a lime — simply because it was unlike any other green in the patch. A few straggling Armenian cucumber vines clung to the net at the back of the garden. I didn't pull them out either, hoping cooler weather would increase the measly production I'd had.

On my last day of intensive gardening before the wedding, I had T come to help me one last time. He'd finally got his passport and was leaving for Australia.

That day, I had a short list for T, but one that would round up my basic garden chores for the season. Earlier in the summer, I'd bought fertilizer spikes for all the trees but had never got around to getting them out of the shed. It was a job Peter had always taken on at our last house, but one I couldn't expect him to do that summer. So I had T go around the yard and knock the spikes in with a hammer at the drip lines of all our evergreens and our wonderful canopy of deciduous trees: the oaks, the ash, the plane, along with the tamarack.

As he pounded away, T told me he planned to come back to Canada in March to work in Niagara the next spring. He already had a job lined up painting houses. And B said she'd wait for him.

He wanted her to come to visit him in Australia, but her difficult ex was unlikely to sign papers that would allow her to travel with their toddler. It all sounded tawdry until I stopped to consider what my life must have looked like from the outside after my marriage had ended and Peter came into our lives when Jane was just three years old.

T worked quickly, but not quickly enough to get everything on my list done. He was more distracted than usual, a man eager to get on with his errands and travels. As we walked to the car, I asked if he was keeping his phone number until the spring. He still hadn't figured that out. What phone he'd keep, what number he'd use; it was all too confusing. His mother had given him an older iPhone to take with him so he could rely on FaceTime to communicate at no cost. His voice rose as he talked about how it would work. "I just have to have Wi-Fi, click, and I can talk to my mom or B."

I may have looked a little bemused, because he added quickly, "I'd heard about it. I just didn't know it was so simple. You just have to click."

He approached me for a hug and I hugged back. I didn't have much in common with this wandering youth except those hours in the garden. But he was the only other person I knew who didn't mind getting covered in mud. I hoped he'd be back in the spring to lessen my workload and entertain me with stories about B and terraforming on another continent.

When I wasn't outside gardening those first days in August, I was in the kitchen. I baked tarts with blueberries from a local Mennonite farm. And I assisted Peter as he made batches of ice cream with local peaches and blueberries. I also baked six savoury tortes for the freezer with Swiss chard from the garden. Even after cutting all the chard leaves I needed, the plants looked untouched. The chard would be on the success side of the garden ledger. So would my Kentucky Wonder beans, which had come through for me once again despite the drought. In the days leading up to our wedding, I found enough beans on the vines to make a salad with mustard dressing that would feed all the guests who wanted it.

On the other side of the yard, in the new bed, the garlic I'd planted after we'd received word of Peter's diagnosis was ready to be harvested. The tops were starting to die back, and when I checked one bulb it came out fat and moist. I carefully dug out the rest of the heads and set my forty-five organic bulbs in a basket to dry for a few days. My faith on that cold November day in garlic's natural ability to survive had paid off. I sat back on the lawn beside the basket and made myself take a moment to admire the bulbs of pink, grey, and white and to appreciate the miracle of their growth. But I soon became distracted by practicalities. I quickly calculated how much garlic to store in the basement for winter, how much to set aside for my fall planting, and how much I would use fresh in the tortes and salads I was making for the wedding.

In the same bed as the garlic, the zucchini had gone from poor to a total writeoff. After I'd harvested small fruit for a few meals and two large ones for bread, the plants stopped producing. I didn't know if there'd been too much dry heat that year or if there hadn't been enough sun in the new garden bed, but alongside the zucchini, small butternut squashes were popping up on vines that circled around trees and flowering plants. They would be my *Cucurbita* success story for the season.

I always go into overdrive when I'm preparing for a group of guests, but in preparation for our wedding, I moved in a mad frenzy, knowing how much this day mattered to us, both in the confirmation of our relationship and as a way of willing a long future together. For weeks, I'd been checking the forecast for the day. When I first started looking, there was nothing but the historic average with a 30 percent chance of rain. As the day grew closer, a high probability of rain was forecast for August fifth and sixth, and then just the sixth or just the fifth, and so on. I, who had been wishing for rain all summer and had been grateful when it finally came, saw rain on our wedding day as a bad omen, not just an inconvenience. But by the middle of the actual week, we knew we'd have a glorious summer day with some of the humidity we'd been suffering through dropping away.

Jane arrived the evening of August third. She'd taken three days off from her job. Her enthusiasm and energy made the final preparations fun. Even though time was getting tight on the day before the wedding, she insisted she and I both go for manicures and pedicures, her idea of what a bride did. Some ideas about tradition had skipped a generation, it seemed. I found the only nail salon in Niagara-on-the-Lake, a shop in the Virgil section of the sprawling town, and we booked the only appointments they had at the end of the day. That morning we finished the final garden touch-ups. While I deadheaded, Jane worked on the grass edging. At one point, in what we all jokingly called her obsessive ways, she gave up on the edging tool and got down on her knees to trim the grass that hung over the flower beds with scissors. Jane had been slow in feeling comfortable in our new house, so removed from Toronto, but in the past year she'd come to appreciate the quiet of the yard and the methodical tasks she could lose herself in. As her love for the garden grew, I felt I was passing on something good to her.

In the late afternoon, after we had all the dishes and glasses organized and the neighbours' chairs and tables on the lawn, we drove to the nail salon, where it became apparent the only woman still there didn't want to bother with us. She said she would have to work on us one at a time and it would take three hours in total.

Even Jane balked at the idea, so we went home and painted our own toenails.

The next morning was a blur of small tasks, but again it was Jane who made me stop for a moment. Together, we wandered the garden collecting hydrangeas of pink, blue, and white for bouquets. I showed her how I'd added the tall, springy gaura to a vase once and she eagerly wanted to include both the pink and white varieties. I've never thought flowers were the hosta's strong suit or even the point of the plant, but Jane loved the thick stems with the pure white buds, so we cut some of those for her bouquet and I added some ferns to mine.

Throughout the morning, we both insisted Peter rest all he could so he would have energy for the afternoon. I had asked TA, the woman who occasionally cleaned our house of the garden dirt I tracked in, to help with the final cleaning jobs that day and to prepare the trays of Prosecco and wine that she, Jane, and my town friend H would serve with hors d'oeuvres when the guests arrived. TA had been coming to us since we moved into the house almost two years earlier. She was a single mother, a clever woman who could have found any number of jobs but took on house-cleaning because when her son had been young she'd needed the flexibility of getting to his school whenever she was wanted. There was much in TA's story I could connect to; I'd certainly sought flexibility in my work when Jane was young. TA had been solicitous when she'd learned of Peter's cancer, and her kindly inquiries had always been comforting.

TA saved the day when she helped Jane and me figure out how to unfold and mount the canopy I'd bought for the service on the lawn in front of the vegetable garden, and she kept the kitchen organized before and after the ceremony. Later, when she left, TA would refuse any payment. Her day of work was part of her wedding gift to us, she said. The other part was a concrete stone with the date of our marriage and our names stamped on it. "I know how much you love your garden," she said when I thanked her.

If the morning went by in a blur, the afternoon went by at hyperspeed. Just as we were finishing laying out the cheese and dessert trays, a bevy of people appeared on our lawn. The event was on. My anxiety over getting things right and over Peter's health gave way to excitement.

Peter was already dressed in his wedding clothes: new pants and jacket with a blue shirt. He'd bought the pants on the July weekend we'd driven through New York State. They were a couple of sizes down from ones he'd worn a year earlier. But when he'd tried the new pants on a few days before the wedding, they'd bunched around his waist. He hadn't wanted me to drive to the mall for a smaller size, so I'd washed them and thrown them in the dryer to try to shrink them. But they were still too large for him on our wedding day. Only his belt kept them in place.

"I hope people don't think I'm dying," he said.

Peter went out to meet our guests while TA, Jane, and H got the trays of drinks and hors d'oeuvres ready. H's husband, A, had come early with her, eager to help. I appointed him wine steward and went out into the yard.

Traffic from Toronto had been heavy and some guests were late arriving, but we finally decided to start the ceremony so our officiant, J, could get on with his day and our guests didn't have to wait too long. I went in the house to change into an off-white tunic. I'd bought the tunic in a mall in Casablanca when I'd been there in June. In the shop's mirror I had looked slim enough in it. But unlike Peter, I had not grown smaller. I'd been stress eating for months, and although for the most part I ate healthily, my middle had grown wider. I could never have imagined that on our wedding day our weights would be so close.

But it was too late to come up with anything else to wear and I forgot my self-consciousness once Jane and I stepped out of the house together with our bouquets to meet Peter under the canopy. If I could stop time, I would stop it for the half hour or so when Jane read "Amazing Grace" in a voice full of emotion, when Peter and I spoke of our love to each other and made our vows. I had insisted on going first because there was never a doubt in my mind that Peter was the more powerful speaker. In my vows, I told Peter that he had always made me laugh, made me think, made my heart grow two sizes bigger every day.

"I have always loved and cherished you," I said as a reminder of vows I'd adhered to if not publicly spoken. "I will always love and cherish you. I have been with you in sickness and health. I will always be with you in sickness and health and through the good and the bad, the times of joy and the times of sorrow. I have always held you. I will always hold you in my heart."

And of course, Peter did speak more eloquently. "To describe myself as a lucky man is to truly beggar the language," he said to the friends and family who had formed a semicircle around the canopy. "Nothing I have done in the past quarter century — becoming a dad, truly learning the meaning of love, travelling the world, learning to walk a third time, confronting cancer, becoming me — none of this would have been possible without the support, companionship, and encouragement of this remarkably generous woman who stands next to me."

He ended by seemingly going off in a direction no one could understand, although those who knew Peter and his long stories well must certainly have known there would be a point eventually. I stood beside Peter, smiling, knowing what that point would be. He described how sixty years before we'd met, astronomer Edwin Hubble had discovered that the universe was expanding.

"All the while we think we are living in a constant. It was not so," he said. "The very structure enveloping us was growing. And this year, appropriately enough, the Hubble telescope gathered data that indicates the expansion of the universe is expanding — the growth is growing upon itself."

In his typical fashion, Peter paused, leaving his audience confused before the aha moment. "You might conceivably wonder why I have wandered off into this odd exploration of astrophysics, but there is a reason. Whenever I have tried to put into words what living with and loving Debi is all about, it always comes down to this. I love her as much as the universe itself and that is constantly expanding."

I closed the few steps between us to kiss Peter, ignoring the officiant's words, "Not yet."

Later, in a backhanded compliment to Peter's vows, a friend of his joked, "You know every man here hates you."

But while Peter had been speaking, I glowed in his words and the depths of his emotions. Perhaps I was a little surprised he shared his private endearment; it felt a little bit as though he wanted it out there while there was time.

I had not included my own endearment, which I often said in response to his. "I love you a bushel" — pause for effect — "*and* a peck." It was the farmer's version, and he understood that for a scrimping farmer to add the peck to the bushel was a big deal. Those endearments always seemed to symbolize the joy of our union, a union between a brilliant man of ideas, philosophy, and soulful searching and a smart woman of the earth and instinct.

During the ceremony Jane forgot to make the recording on her phone she said she'd make. We'd all forgot to cut a fresh rosebud for Peter's lapel before the ceremony. And after, I forgot to get a photograph of Peter and me alone because I wanted to get the buffet ready for the guests and I could see he was tired and wanted to sit down. Later, I'd make an album of the photographs that were taken by friends and came to accept them as the record of the day, even if the netting for the peas and the tomato stakes appeared in the background, even if my vain streak found my skin and hair too white in the bright afternoon sun. But none of what didn't happen mattered in the end. We were all happy about what did happen that afternoon.

After Jane went back to Toronto the next day, Peter and I settled in for a relaxing end to the summer. He booked us tickets for plays at the Shaw Festival. We made a list of activities we wanted to do before the warm weather ended. We had a social calendar for the first time in a while. D, the octogenarian sexton of the local Anglican church, a man who takes pleasure in his town and his life to heights I've rarely seen, invited Peter and me over to dinner. We sat in his lush garden as the light dimmed and the crickets chirped, in a magical space that made me feel I was somewhere in the Deep South, while two Scotties with muddy paws jumped all over my off-white linen pants. D and his friend, also D, had heard of our wedding and feted us with pink roses from the famous rose grower in town and joked about the newlyweds. I had warned them both that Peter wouldn't eat much, but even so they both looked shocked at the serving Peter took, which covered one small corner of his plate.

Two days later we went to a *cinq à sept*. Having people over for late-afternoon drinks on a Friday, we'd learned, is a popular way of getting together in Niagara-on-the-Lake. This time we went to the refurbished house of a man whom I'd met on my press trip to Spain. Both he and his wife were in their seventies, swam at a hotel pool each morning, and walked hand in hand around town after days spent writing. Their home in the older part of town was eclectic and filled with sunny art and books. We knew they were people we'd like to know better.

They were both vegetarians who only ate organic. I'd already given them yellow beets and chard from my garden and that day took them a basket filled with carrots, more beets, tomatoes, kale, and more chard. I liked taking produce as gifts and that year, especially, filling a basket for someone else rarely made a dent. We followed up with emails that ended with an invitation to visit them in their home in Santa Fe that fall if we could.

Visiting and travels were much on our minds. Peter was working on the idea of doing two radio documentaries for CBC during our month in Rome. He had the flights booked, as well as a small apartment in the Trastevere neighbourhood. And we talked about taking a driving trip in September to Washington, D.C., to visit friends and see the Victory Garden at the Smithsonian. We both assumed, or perhaps just wished, that Peter's problems with eating and back pain would end soon.

When we weren't planning or socializing, we sat on our deck admiring a garden that now gave me a reprieve. By mid-August, the tasks in the garden were fewer. I could do as much or as little as I wanted. I even spent one afternoon reading in the hammock under the trees at the back of the yard.

Soon enough, though, the Victory Garden could not be ignored. The beans became prolific, so I blanched enough for winter soups and got them in the freezer. The tomatoes, once they took to ripening, came on fast. Since the wedding, it had rained often enough that they had doubled in size, leaving stretch marks at one end. Each day I picked the Romas and spread them out on the counter in the basement. Each day, more turned red. I made my first batch of tomato sauce with carrots, garlic, and basil from the garden and local onions. I also bought local corn, which I cooked and stripped the niblets from for the freezer. Usually about this time, Peter would be preparing small packs of pesto for the winter, too, but he hadn't got through the last summer's supply and showed no interest in making the sauce he loved so much.

Even as I squirrelled away food for the cold months, I wondered why I was doing it. Each time I opened the freezer door, bags of zucchini and banana muffins we'd baked rolled out. We liked to take the muffins in the car or on the GO Train when we went into Toronto so Peter would have something to eat every two hours, but he hadn't wanted any of the muffins in a while.

In the middle of August, in the midst of all my cooking, we drove to Hamilton for Peter's second CT scan. We felt no great anxiety the day he got it or during the wait for the results; the first one in May had been clear, and since all of Peter's symptoms matched everything we'd learned about his recovery, we saw no reason to fear that this one would show any cancer.

The Sunday after the scan, I turned to the second phase of the Victory Garden: planting radishes, lettuce, and spinach for fall crops. And I tried to see if I could revitalize the zucchini. I fed the plants with Muskie Fish Emulsion Fertilizer, recommended for tomatoes by M, a successful urban gardener I knew. One plant in the bed appeared to be rotten where the stem met the root, so I pulled it up, only to discover it led to a long, vibrantly green vine of butternut squash that supported two decently sized squash and several baby ones. I made my lunch that day with a stir-fry from the garden of tomatoes that needed to be used, orange and yellow carrots, green beans, and beet greens. I topped the dish with the baby squash and fresh Thai basil. It was the way I loved to eat in the summer. It was the victory of growing my own vegetables. But the victory felt hollow. I knew I was nourishing myself. I just didn't know how to nourish Peter.

And his eating problems were getting to him. Throughout the cancer treatment, Peter had displayed his usual steely resolve to do what had to be done. But we just hadn't been expecting what he was going through now. There seemed no single goal here; the answers were elusive. His digestive system wouldn't behave and he had continuous stomach cramps or bloating. And I didn't know how to help. But I worried he was sinking into a form of depression I'd only seen him go through after his father died and as his arthritis grew more debilitating before the orthopedic surgery gave him new hope for a long, fruitful life and the incentive to travel again and move to our new home.

One day that week, as Peter was drinking chocolate milk, a fly flew into his glass. He seemed to take it personally, as if the world were out to get him. I didn't like him thinking that way. And I finally said something about it. I said he had been through so much and none of it was fair, but if he let himself fall into a downward spiral, it would only make things worse. One small victory we'd gained in our communications that year was in saying openly what we thought and accepting what we heard. Time was too precious for holding back or resenting honestly spoken words. Peter thanked me for the reminder.

His eating problems were affecting me, too. As I planted the radish seeds, I wondered why I was bothering growing more food. But then as I stood in the garden, I admired the miracle of how the leaves curled around a cabbage plant, swirling to form a head. It was a beautiful thing. And as I watered the radish seeds I remembered a saying I'd come across: "They tried to bury us. They didn't know we were seeds." We were a defiant couple.

On the Monday, I baked. I don't bake much; Peter has always been the baker in the house. Before he got sick, he would bake a loaf of sourdough bread every week from starter we kept in the fridge. I'd thrown the starter out in the fall when Peter stopped eating bread, because the jar of starter just kept getting bigger each time I fed it. Containers of different flours still sat in the pantry. I hadn't had the heart to throw them out yet.

The blueberry tarts had disappeared quickly at the wedding before Peter had been able to get one, and he expressed regret that he hadn't tasted them. So, I decided to make more for him, hoping to find something he could enjoy. The kitchen counter was covered with unrolled pastry and flour that Monday morning, the twenty-second of August, when Peter's cellphone rang. After the CT the week before, he had phoned Dr. F's office pushing for an early follow-up appointment. He wanted to get a referral to the best gastroenterologist in Hamilton to tackle his digestive issues. He wanted to be well for Rome in November. As he'd sat on the deck that morning, he'd cried, exhausted by the constant pain in his gut or his back.

It was Dr. F's assistant on the phone, who said the only clinic that week was that day and asked if he could be there by three. I nodded that we could and hurried to finish my baking.

Even so, I got us there a few minutes late, and by the time I'd parked the car, Peter was in the waiting area. A resident, Dr. P, called us into a room soon after. I didn't really listen to him at first when he asked Peter questions; residents are just the set-up for the doctor, after all.

"Call me Jon or Jonathan, whichever you prefer," he said, before taking a list of Peter's symptoms. He didn't seem to want to hear them, though. I found that frustrating until I realized he was preparing himself for what he had to say. "Unfortunately," he said, "the tumour is back. And it's pressing against your heart and your spine."

Neither Peter nor I visibly reacted, our minds still ready to fight for action on the gut issues.

"You were all right at first after the surgery," the resident said, and I didn't listen after that. He left us then, saying Dr. F would be in. We held hands, with tears in our eyes and few words on our lips as we waited.

"Well, at least we have an explanation for my back pain," Peter finally said.

"Yes," I answered. "But not the one we wanted to hear."

"Hey, buddy," Dr. F said when he came in the room. His usual greeting. He repeated the news and said that what had been a spot that had worried him on the first scan was now an eight-centimetre mass that had grown fast. He'd never mentioned the spot before; we'd never completely understood the nature of his worry. Nor had the oncologists Dr. S or Dr. D, who seemed to think everything looked fine based on the first scan and the pathologist's report. But I was too stunned to query Dr. F.

He stayed with us only for a few moments. "I'm sorry," he said, and I was grateful he didn't blather on about his own regrets. He couldn't operate on the tumour because of its location between the heart and spine. All he could do was send us back to the Juravinski Cancer Centre for more radiation and chemo.

"But Dr. S said he can't have more radiation," I said.

"This is different," he answered.

"So it's metasti—?" I didn't get the full word out because I wasn't sure I would say it correctly.

"Yes," he said.

Just as I'd had to learn how to spell *esophagus* without hesitating in the winter, I now had to learn to write and say *metastasize*. Words that had seemed like vocabulary I could ignore became intimates in a moment.

"How long do I have?" Peter asked. My gut involuntarily shuddered at the question.

"Could be weeks, could be months, could be a year or two," Dr. F answered. "There are those who live for several years. It's hard to say."

Even though Peter's shock must have been more intense than mine, he transitioned smoothly into his helpful mode, offering to send Dr. F a link to a clinical study that showed how bad doctors were at predicting the length of life remaining for terminally ill patients. The two discussed the methodology of the study while I shook my head.

"How was your summer?" Peter asked. "Did you get some time off?"

Dr. F nodded. "You're a gracious man," he said.

We left the office with a prescription for an opioid to ease Peter's back pain and a reminder to call if we needed anything from Dr. F. As I walked to get the car, the sunny summer day and the normalness of the city streets jarred with my emotions. I wanted to cry but had to hold it together to get us home safely. Being strong, being a caregiver, comes at the cost of pushing down emotions. But I couldn't push everything down. There was the real probability that I would lose Peter, that I would be alone. It was unthinkable that such a bright, kind human so full of ideas and plans could vanish. That there could be a day as beautiful as this one without Peter there to witness it.

On the way home, we both cried as we moved through traffic on the Queen Elizabeth Way. "I have so much I want to do," Peter said. There could still be some time, we both said. Maybe he'd never be an eighty-year-old man, but maybe he'd be a sixty-five- or a sixty-seven-year-old one. Maybe he'd have to decide which book he wanted to write most. By the time we got close to home, we had the lifespan bumped up to seventy and the books down to two thrillers that had been rattling around in his brain.

"Now, this doesn't stop your Victory Garden project," Peter said sternly. It was a generous thing to say, but I couldn't read the subtext. Was he saying there would be another victory for him or that, if the cancer defeated him, I would have to find my own victory? I didn't ask. Perhaps I didn't want the answer.

When we got home, I had no wish to tell anyone the news, especially Jane, who had been so happy at our wedding. When

Peter had received his first diagnosis, he'd immediately taken to his blog and I'd had to hurry to get emails and calls to the people I felt shouldn't find out that way.

"Please don't blog about this tonight," I said. I didn't have the energy to get ahead of any news he'd post. But it seemed he had no appetite for sharing the news either. We both needed to sit with it first.

We wanted this story to have ended. We'd gone through terrifying uncertainty in the winter and after Peter's frightening surgery. We were in a period of slow recovery. The end. Peter and Debi get on with their lives. Peter's a hit as the moderator at three local author events in a series called Wine and Words. Peter produces a six-part series for CBC *Ideas*. (Wow, isn't he productive!) Peter and Debi write books. Peter and Debi go to Rome. Peter and Debi stay in their home and watch their trees grow over the years. The end. The end. The end we'd told ourselves and shared with others. How could we tell Jane, how could we tell anyone, the story had taken a different turn?

We sat on our deck, staring at our gorgeous garden in the soft late-afternoon light while we agonized over how to give the news to Jane. We admired our trees one moment and talked about cancer the next. Had the cancer metastasized if it wasn't in an organ? You hear so much about it turning up in the lungs or liver. We stretched for any good news. Peter searched "metastasized" on Google and said it meant cancer cells had moved through the lymph system or the blood to another part of the body.

Restless, I got up and walked around the garden. I admired the tall purple delphiniums, the yellow saucer-sized flowers of the hibiscus tree I'd bought for next to nothing at an end-of-season sale. None of them gave my any happiness. *We got nothing*, they seemed to say. I stared at the rows in my Victory Garden where I'd planted seeds the day before. Were they already opening and starting to germinate, indifferent to our pain? In the squash patch, I studied the zucchini plants, needing some sign a zucchini was developing but found none.

That night I woke up thinking of the butternut squash plant I'd pulled up the day before, the one with the rotting root and the healthy vine that stretched to the end of the garden. And it made me think of metastasizing, of spreading out and settling somewhere else. Never had my garden seemed so malevolent.

The next day we both felt a little stronger. I made a soup from the butternut squash for Peter and a supper for me of rigatoni with beet greens, red onion, sliced Romas, and garlic from the garden. It had become my routine to plan my meals around the vegetables available in the garden. In the mornings, I sautéed a chopped tomato or two with a cup of basil and threw in an egg and Parmesan to hold the mixture together. At lunch, I'd make a toasted tomato sandwich or a Greek salad. At supper I'd cook all the vegetables I could handle in various dishes. Those meals gave me moments of such pleasure. Meanwhile, Peter kept to old favourites of his own like chicken pot pie and tourtière. He seemed to crave meat more than ever.

That day, we agreed that if we had to go somewhere for treatment again, we were both pleased it would be the Juravinski Cancer Centre. The team there had always been efficient and open to questions. Cancer is a manageable disease, we told ourselves. We'd have to think in those terms. Peter got a call to go to Dr. D, the chemotherapy oncologist at the Juravinski, the following Tuesday. As we'd expected, further radiation was out of the question.

We knew we had to tell Jane soon, but didn't want to call her when there was only fear and no plan. We thought it might be easier to tell her face to face, so Peter texted her to say we had to go to Toronto and to ask whether she be available for dinner on Wednesday or Thursday. She wasn't free either evening. We didn't want to keep suggesting days and raise suspicions, so we decided to wait until after our appointment when we could say, "Here's what's going to happen."

Sitting on the deck that evening, I thought of a meme I'd seen on Facebook that has Charlie Brown saying, "Some day we will all die," and Snoopy answering, "True, but on all the other days we live."

The next morning, with the pink roses from D and D fading, I went out to pick fresh flowers for the house. I sent Jane a picture of the mix of hydrangeas, delphiniums, butterfly bush flowers, and hostas, and she texted back that hydrangeas would always remind her of our wedding. I hoped that would be true, that our wedding would be her most important memory of that summer. When I walked past the vegetable bed, I noticed something red peeking out from between the tomatoes and the chard. I thought at first it was a tomato stretching into the row of pepper plants, but no, it was a gorgeous, plump red pepper. The Redstart peppers I'd started from seed in the spring were doing their job. There were four of them hidden under leaves, and as I pulled them from the plants a pang of joy jolted me. Others before me had successfully grown red peppers, but I never had. New things were still possible.

Peter was still upstairs in the bedroom. I went up to him with an idea. Let's use our wedding date as a goal, get to six months, then a year, and each time have our own quiet celebration. He said he liked the idea, and we decided to first set a modest goal of three months: get to November sixth — to garlic-planting time in garden terms. I pictured us raising our glasses once the cloves were ensconced underground.

In bed that night, I rubbed his back and threw my arm around him. "I don't want to lose you," I said. Was I trying to give him encouragement to go on or was I just being selfish? I don't know. I know I needed him to understand how essential he was to my existence.

I moved through the rest of the week in a mix of tears, anxiety, and imagining. Although I wanted to stop myself, I couldn't help but wonder what I'd do if I were alone. I'd stay in this house, I decided, for at least another garden season. Perhaps I'd end up as the crazy old lady down the street with the beautiful garden. But I hated myself for those thoughts.

In the cool mornings, I rearranged flower beds or weeded the vegetable garden, losing myself in the work. I have always hated the arrival of the dark days and the cold weather, and as the sun finally grew in strength by midmorning, I realized how tough the next winter would be. The trip to Rome was meant to ease us over the hump, to keep my November depression over the coming of the dark days at bay. We had decided to wait until after our meeting with Dr. D to cancel the trip, but I think we both knew we were kidding ourselves.

The hydromorphone Peter was now taking made his digestive problems even worse. He felt bloated and constipated all the time. And it seemed to take all motivation away from him. He didn't want to go to the gym, which frightened me. Before Peter had his orthopedic surgery in 2012, he'd known he had to keep up his walking before the long period of his recovery. And he walked even though each step he took sent excruciating pain up his leg. By then, the silver plate from his operation as a boy, a plate that held his leg to his hip, was causing striations in his pelvis. Nonetheless, each day we'd drive to the park that ran along the Humber River near our Toronto home and he'd walk, marking how far he had to go by walking to an old willow tree that he loved and back to the parked car. After his surgery, in the year he'd learned to walk again, he'd stubbornly worked on his walking once the nerves in his leg had settled down and he could get off his crutches.

He'd shown that same determination in his first round of cancer treatment. We'd go to the gym near our new home, and after some exercises to keep up his muscle mass, he'd walk on the indoor track that circled the areas for weights and machines and the elevator shaft. As I did weights, I'd hear the click of his cane getting closer and closer before seeing him come around the corner at a hearty clip.

But in the time since his cancer surgery, he'd lost much of the muscle in his arms and legs; his once-strong thighs were like sticks. I fretted over how he'd get through another round of treatments. One day, I persuaded him to go to the gym, and while I worked with weights he started the circle. When I no longer could hear his cane, I wondered what had happened. I found him sitting by a window at the other end of the gym.

"I've had enough," he said casually, as if walking was a slight matter. He couldn't have gone more than three times around the track. Three times around the track was not enough.

That week, two thumb-sized zucchini appeared on a vine, but within a day they both withered away. Victory seemed so unlikely.

Finally, the day for the visit to Dr. D arrived. While we were both afraid she might say there was nothing she could do, we took some comfort in knowing the driving route to the Juravinski in Hamilton by heart. During the first panicked visits in the fall, I'd driven around the neighbourhood for half an hour before settling on the cheapest street parking I could find. This time I knew exactly where to park. Even in the darkest times, the smallest things offer sparks of reassurance.

Everyone who saw Peter — the assistant, the nurse, and Dr. D herself — was alarmed at his weight loss. On their scale, he weighed in at 145, down from the 187 pounds recorded during his follow-up visit in the spring, down from slightly more than 200 when the cancer was first diagnosed. Dr. D reminded us that chemotherapy was the only option, but it could never destroy the tumour; it could only shrink it and give Peter six to eighteen months more of life. Neither of us brought up how wrong doctors could be, but I'm sure it was in the back of Peter's mind, as it was in mine. When he'd had his blood problems, the doctor had described Peter as "a tank" for living with his low hemoglobin count. Even though Peter didn't look like a tank now, part of me still thought of him as a survivor.

Dr. D wasn't prepared to start the treatment she proposed — two intravenous chemo drugs and one in the form of tablets — until she knew the state of Peter's heart because one of the drugs was hard on the heart. She ordered an echocardiogram. She also wanted a feeding tube in Peter to keep his weight steady, and that would mean waiting for a surgical bed. And she ordered blood work to make sure he didn't have an infection. It was best to have everything in order before beginning, she said, so the negative effects of the drugs didn't outweigh the benefits. If everything wasn't in order, she said, Peter could end up in hospital with septic shock and they'd have to wait to start the chemotherapy again. She also warned he shouldn't be sedentary for more than 50 percent of the time, and I fretted again about Peter's lack of interest in exercise.

That night, we finally found the courage to call Jane. The cancer has returned, we said. They are going to try chemo. Kept it simple until we could see her in person. She told us she was coming for the Labour Day weekend and could come early since there was no work at her job in the city hall courts in the days before the long weekend.

The next evening, I drove along the Lakeshore to pick her up at the bus stop in St. Catharines, past the fruit stands, the orchards, and the vineyards of Niagara, a region that was in my soul. I rolled down the windows for the cool breeze, rolled up the volume on the radio. The song was Justin Bieber's hit "Sorry." The adult in me issued instructions to turn the radio off or listen to something more intelligent, more inspiring. The teenager in me relived summer evening drives after a day of farm work with the latest hit *du jour* blasting out of the car and life full of possibilities. The teenager won out.

I revelled in the drive and later revelled in an evening with Jane as we ate rigatoni with red peppers, Swiss chard, and my latest batch of tomato sauce, as we drank red wine and watched the feel-good movie *Chef.* This was the calm I'd been seeking over the past week, but it left me feeling guilty.

Peter was in bed but awake when I went upstairs. Selfishly, I cried when he asked if we'd had a good evening and I told him we had. "Don't," he said. "You're allowed to have a good time. I wouldn't want you not to."

After the fall of France in the Second World War, Britain's prime minister Winston Churchill called it the "darkest hour," referring to a line by Thomas Fuller: "It is always darkest just before the Day dawneth." But how does one find the courage to go on, to patiently wait for doctors to try new treatments, to continue digging and planting, when victory looks unlikely, when the dawn could bring harsher news? All I knew that evening, as summer was coming to an end, was that it was all going to hurt so much.

Chapter Thirteen

LABOUR DAY WEEKEND OFFERED US a gift that year: breathing space of golden days and warm evenings. In the garden, the flower beds were still vibrantly coloured by coneflowers, roses, and coreopsis, and the vegetable patch was showing off with produce ready for the plucking. Tomatoes still ripened; bean flowers still blossomed; the chard and the kale showed no signs of giving up. Jane had come home and was willing to help in the garden. Peter sat on the deck, on the orange cushions of his wicker chair.

It would have been enough, under normal circumstances, to have me humming Crosby, Stills, Nash, and Young's "Our House," but while the picture of the three of us in our yard looked peaceful enough, unseen shadows, like tumours on a CT scan, clouded our thoughts, weighed down our hearts. On Friday, Peter received news of an appointment to install a feeding tube on September nineteenth, three long weeks away. His tumour had grown from a spot to eight centimetres between May and the middle of August. It was hard not to imagine it was still growing like an overripe zucchini forgotten in the garden. We had hoped treatments that would shrink the tumour, if not get rid of it, would begin within a week or two. But Dr. D insisted she couldn't begin chemotherapy until the feeding tube was in place. She was also waiting on the results of the echocardiogram. It all made sense — there was no use starting chemotherapy if Peter's body couldn't withstand the treatment — but the wait was tortuous nonetheless.

The wicker chair had become Peter's default location in the late summer as his energy waned with the summer light. From the chair, he stared out at the canopy of trees at the back of the yard. He could, he often said, stare at trees for hours and zone out, just as he had done in what he called "the loneliest year of my life," that year in a bed at the back of a suburban house. That Labour Day weekend, he zoned out for hours.

My memories of the Peter of the past, sitting in chairs on decks, are of a robust man sipping coffee and deep into a thick book, chuckling at one line, nodding his head at the insight of another. He was the man, after all, who on our first family vacation together brought a thick hardcover biography of Dickens as his light cottage reading. But this Peter had lost his appetite for coffee and food, as well as his concentration for burrowing into the weighty tomes he favoured. The hydromorphone, prescribed by Dr. F for Peter's back pain, fogged his brain as it continued to worsen his digestive system.

After his surgery in February, Peter couldn't wait to get rid of his feeding tube. In his typical stubborn fashion, he ate his small meals religiously until the dietitian decided the tube — never used outside of the hospital — could be removed. Now, we were both desperate for him to have another one.

On that heart-stopping visit when we'd learned the cancer had returned, Dr. F had said that if there was ever anything he could do, Peter should not hesitate to call him. Dr. F was a surgeon. A surgeon should be able to pull some strings to get a surgical bed earlier than the nineteenth, we reasoned. Peter drafted an email requesting Dr. F's help. The Peter I knew would have written such an email in minutes and maybe run it by me to make sure the tone was all right, but this Peter relied on Jane and me to help him compose paragraphs that were merely cogent.

With the email sent, we tried to make the most of our weekend together.

On Sunday, we had a near-average day. I made a breakfast of eggs, bacon, and garden tomatoes. Peter ate one poached egg on a piece of toast with half a piece of bacon crumbled on top and he seemed to enjoy it. He and Jane sat reading while I planted another evergreen near the chain-link fence at the side of our property closest to the deck. Slowly, I'd been creating a living wall with the existing ivy that clung to the fence by adding more and more evergreens and euonymus to hide a swimming pool on the other side. Our neighbours of two years, quiet, kind people, were moving to another town, and we weren't sure who would be moving in or whether they'd use the house themselves or rent it out as so many in our town did. I was afraid we'd lose our privacy and the silence of our yard. Peter warned me, once again, not to get ahead of the story. But he was always happy to see another tree and smiled in approval when I'd finished the job.

We saw little reason to leave our home that weekend. We were outside most of the day. Inside, I wrote emails to people who didn't know yet that Peter's cancer had returned and made another batch of tomato sauce for winter. Suppers were easy. I cooked whatever Peter wanted and made Jane and me stir-fried vegetables with brown rice, and grilled chicken with more vegetables. Once darkness came, Jane and I walked through the streets of the town with only the sound of crickets around us.

"Mom," she said one evening, "you know you can call me whenever you want. I'm tougher than you think."

Labour Day Monday was Jane's last day with us. She and I got up early and drove to the Niagara River gorge, where, in the spring, we had climbed down to the rocky shore that encircled swirling, deep blue waters. As we hiked, Jane railed against the injustice of a world that had given Peter so much pain.

"How many times does he have to go through this?" she asked. "It isn't fair."

I had no answer. I had been finding it especially cruel that the tumour was encroaching on the two areas of Peter's body that had never given him trouble: his back and his heart. Jane's anger reminded me of my own, and of a video I'd seen on Facebook. An interviewer asked the British comedian Stephen Fry what he'd say if he ever met God at the pearly gates. And Fry had let it rip. He had no truck with a god that gave children bone cancer and made people kneel before him while there was so much injustice and suffering in the world. Watching Fry's indignation had been cathartic, so I listened as Jane ranted, hoping that would ease her suffering, too.

Later, in the afternoon, Jane came into the great room where Peter sat in his favourite chair. She told him she was feeling sad. He gave her the same advice he and I had been giving each other: We had to give ourselves moments to be sad and angry. But we also had to remember we had so much good in our lives.

"Don't you ever think it's unfair?" she asked him.

"I have so much that so many people could never have," he answered her, gesturing to the garden past the windows.

He made it clear he wasn't giving up. He told us both that evening he was working on an outline for his thriller.

"When can we see it?" Jane asked.

"I'll send it to you both by the end of the week."

Before I took Jane to catch her train, I made our traditional end-of-summer treat, bruschetta with olive oil and tomatoes, basil, garlic, and a bit of red onion, all from the garden. I always add a dash of sea salt and a splash of balsamic vinegar. It's a recipe we all liked. Whenever we ordered bruschetta in a restaurant, Jane or Peter or both would say, "It's good, but yours is better."

That evening, I scooped the mixture onto Melba canapés instead of grilled bread, hoping Peter could eat more pieces that way. Even so, he ate only some of the topping from one piece while Jane and I hurriedly ate the rest. I bit down on my disappointment. When I'd come up with the idea of creating a Victory Garden the previous fall, the image I'd carried in my head for months was of such a summer evening with the three of us savouring our favourite appetizer, with Peter free of cancer, his appetite for food and life strong.

Two days later I faced a dilemma. We had no news about the feeding tube or the condition of Peter's heart. We were no closer to treatment. I had a meeting in Toronto that afternoon with my group of supportive and talented women writers. It was a meeting I'd come to think of as essential, and I knew I'd probably have to miss other times once Peter started treatment or, if worst came to worst, there was nothing more that could be done for him.

That morning, Peter was on the deck. When he wasn't staring out into the yard, he dozed, his head bent. When I came out with a coffee, he encouraged me to go to Toronto, said that he had his phone in his pocket if anyone called, that he'd be all right, that he'd ask our neighbours for help if he needed anything. He said he'd made a call to the nurse who worked with Dr. D to see if there was something stronger than the laxatives he was using to get his digestive system working and he'd text me when he heard back and let me know if I needed to pick up any medication on the way home. I had given him the chapter I'd written about the garden and our lives in August that I was going to pass out to my group, and I asked him if there was anything he didn't want me to include.

"No," he said. "It's your story."

I wasn't convinced.

"But is there anything you don't want me saying about you?"

"No," he answered. "I'm fine with it all. It's good."

I got to the meeting in record time but felt distracted, impatient to get back on the road and home. I left early enough to avoid rush hour, I thought, but I still hit heavy traffic that made my progress slow and my heart race with worry. Peter had texted to say he was fine and there'd been no news. I stopped in Grimsby to pick up a few foods that he still enjoyed. There was a good antibiotic-free chicken pot pie and I texted him to see if he wanted it. By the time I got home, I was so famished I thought I'd put it in the oven for both of us.

But Peter didn't want any of it. He said he wasn't hungry; he was feeling too gassy to eat. He suggested I cook the pie and he'd eat the leftovers for lunch the next day. I didn't bother — said I'd bake it fresh for him the next day — and began to put the groceries away and fuss with some laundry. I watched Peter get up and go to the small washroom off our great room. Then I heard a groan.

"What is it?" I asked through the closed door.

He came out almost staggering and I could hear him wheezing. I worried that the trouble with his digestive system had reached a critical level. Neither of us had wanted to take him to emergency, where he'd have to repeat his medical history yet again, be probed by doctors intrigued by his past. As had happened every time he'd had to go to the hospital.

He had kept telling me he felt like his body would work again soon, but now, with one look at him, I knew something horrible was happening. "Should I get you to the hospital?" I said.

"Give me a few minutes," he answered and walked back to his chair. But he'd barely sat down before he said, "Call an ambulance."

I told the ambulance dispatcher my husband was in distress and gave her a quick summary of what Peter had been going through.

"Is he hot or clammy?" she asked.

I rushed over to touch Peter's forehead. "Clammy," I said.

Peter sighed irritably and the dispatcher said an ambulance was on its way. Past his chair, I could see the garden through the large picture window, looking normal, calm, and beautiful. It might as well have been a distant planet. Peter continued to groan.

"They're on their way," I told him, which made him grunt more. He always hated when people said things like "We're almost there."

I didn't know what was happening to him, but he didn't seem to want to talk and I didn't push for answers. I walked to the front door several times, and after what seemed like just a few minutes, saw the ambulance in our driveway. Peter was impatient with the attendants as they attached cords to him and tried to get him to stand up. They pushed furniture out of the way before they supported him to the stretcher.

"I'm feeling incontinent," he said and somehow the accuracy of his vocabulary made me think he would be all right.

"It doesn't matter," one of the two attendants said.

Peter argued with them as they tried to buckle him into the stretcher. "I don't want to lie down," he said angrily.

"Sir, you have to lie back before we can put you in the ambulance." The male attendant turned to me then and told me to gather Peter's meds for them and then follow the ambulance in my car to the hospital. "Take your time. Drive carefully."

By the time I had the medications and Peter's health card in a bag, they had won the argument and were wheeling Peter out the front door. I followed and saw my neighbour M cross the street. She hugged me, and before I could tell her what was going on, the female driver hopped out of the ambulance and said, "The way he's presenting, you should come with us."

I nodded and went back into the house for a bottle of water because my throat was parched, and then I stopped to lock the front door. "C'mon," the driver said, rolling her eyes. It was only when I walked to the passenger side of the ambulance that I saw the male attendant pumping Peter's chest through the back doors.

With the siren whining, we drove down our street and onto the highway to the hospital in St. Catharines. The female driver used her radio to request assistance of some kind. A television monitor at the top of the windshield showed Peter on the stretcher in the back and the attendant bent over him. "Peter, Peter," the attendant said repeatedly as he massaged Peter's heart.

"Has his heart stopped?" I asked the driver. I asked the question as if I were someone else, not as someone whose loved one could be dying, not as someone whose life could soon be shattered.

The attendant was vague, or maybe I didn't want to hear her. Instead, my practical side kicked in. Jane needed to be here; I had to tell Jane what was going on and figure out a way to get her to the hospital. I phoned her and told her I was in an ambulance and Peter wasn't doing well. Then I called my brother in Toronto to see if he could pick her up and bring her to me. He had guests and had had a couple of drinks, it turned out, but my niece was there and she offered to drive Jane. I called our new friends in town, H and A, and left a message.

Halfway down the highway, the attendant in the back asked the driver to stop and come help him. With the siren still on, the red light spreading patterns over the hood, I sat alone in the front staring at the monitor with the two bent over Peter in the back. Another ambulance pulled in behind them and a third attendant climbed into the back.

I called Jane to tell her about the pickup arrangements; I tried to keep the fear from my voice. How was I able to act so calmly when everything seemed to be falling apart? Was I incapable of really living this moment? I felt like I was in a movie of someone else's life. From my high vantage point in the ambulance, I watched cars drive by, measured the looks on faces. Were they sympathetic, curious, averse to noticing the drama? It somehow offended me that they didn't seem to care about me or Peter, although I'm certain I've passed many ambulances with the same disregard.

Then we were back on the road. In an attempt to stay in control, I talked to the driver about her route, which didn't seem the shortest way to the hospital to me. She said it was the one where she was most unlikely to encounter traffic, so I sat back quietly staring up at the monitor, the attendant still massaging Peter's heart. I tried to send Peter silent messages. *Hang in there. I'm here with you.* We hadn't had a moment at the house to say anything real to each other.

When we pulled up to the emergency department and I stepped out of the ambulance, attendants were already rushing to the back door and a man in green scrubs came up to me. "Does he have a do-not-resuscitate order?"

I stood stock-still. "What? We've never talked about end-of-life issues." I paused before adding, "But he wants to fight this cancer, so do what you can." I didn't ask what that involved or what state Peter was in. Sometimes I just don't ask the right questions, but the man in green seemed to accept my answer and hospital staff whisked Peter away.

Someone ushered me into a small room in the emergency wing where the ambulance driver and a nurse came to sit with me. I tried to converse. "What is your name?" I asked the driver.

"Taylor," she answered. An odd name for a woman, I thought, but I didn't ask why she'd been given it. I was all out of questions.

The man in green came into the room and sat across from me. He was the emergency doctor, a young man with a Muslim name on his tag. Irrationally, I wanted to tell him that I'd written a book about Muslim refugees, that I wasn't anti-Muslim. As if somehow, if he liked me, he could perform a miracle. Thankfully, I kept my mouth shut. Some filters were still working. The doctor told me they had started Peter's heart, but the procedure was quite violent and they had broken some ribs. And I wondered what I had done.

"I know you can't advise me," I said before the doctor could say anything else. I wanted his advice; I needed some guidance.

"Yes, I can," he said hurriedly. I waited. "We can keep his heart going," he said, "but the outcome will be the same. His heart is likely damaged and he's probably suffered neurological damage." I didn't hear all his other words, but "will not recover" was among them. *Will not recover.* In other words, will die or be in some horrible state. It was the idea of neurological damage that disturbed me most. *Not his brain. Not his brain. His heart, his back, and now his brain.* He was a brilliant man. His inquisitive, analytical, absorbing mind had given him great joy in life, eased his suffering through the worst of times, earned him the greatest respect. I couldn't leave him this way.

We must be capable of computer-speed calculations in such moments. I thought of Jane and whether I should keep Peter alive until she got there. I thought of the added pain I might have caused Peter. I thought of how he would hate to know his brain was damaged. And I came to a decision in a flash. I told the doctor I wanted their interference stopped and I wanted to be with Peter. He told me to give them a few minutes and then I could sit beside Peter until he died and as long after as I wanted.

Peter was lying on a bed, covered with a blanket up to the top of his chest. His mouth was open and there was blood around the corners of his lips. The nurse wiped his mouth before she left me alone with him. Peter's favourite summer shirt, white with a blue and brown criss-cross pattern, had been cut with scissors; it bunched up around his neck. It was a shirt that popped up in our travel photos from warm places. In the best shot I'd taken of Peter on our Santa Fe trip, he'd been wearing that shirt with one side of the collar poking out over a blue sweater that matched his eyes, smiling at me with deep love.

But it was his face that struck me most when I sat down beside him. It had yellowed, to be sure, but there was not a single wrinkle on it. In the past months, as he'd lost weight, the heavy wrinkles of a man much older than he was had formed around his eyes and mouth. To say he finally looked at peace is a cliché, but it was a true one.

I wasn't aware of his breathing, but when I sat beside him and held his hand, it was warm. For years, on winter nights before cancer made his body colder than mine, I would sneak my frigid feet over to his side of the bed and warm them against his calves. He would shiver in mock horror but never protest. Now I stroked his warm hand and drew strength from it. Even though I am not a religious person, I knew that, if there are souls, Peter had an old one, one that had become wise and had known much.

I sat there on automatic, trying to do what I thought I had to do without feeling anything. I spoke to Peter and told him I had to let him go, that I loved him but he should go peacefully. He was unconscious, near death, but I said the words aloud anyway. In case he could hear; in case they were words he had to hear.

At some point, perhaps about twenty minutes later, the nurse came into the room. "Is he dead?" I asked. I hadn't noticed an end to his breathing. And his hand was still warm.

"About five minutes ago," she said. She stopped the drip of hydromorphone and left the room again. Was his soul leaving his body? Was there a presence in the room? I said goodbye, told him it was all right, again just in case. I had been with both my parents when they'd died and had said similar words. Those words had brought me some relief then, had made some sense to me. My parents had been elderly, had gone to church, lived full lives, and

I felt I was supporting them through a necessary passage. I wanted to give Peter the same support, but in my heart, I felt cold, false. I'd been cheated. He'd been cheated. We'd both been cheated. Death had come too early and too suddenly. We hadn't even had a chance to say goodbye. But I wouldn't let the anger overwhelm me. I had to keep doing what I was supposed to do when a loved one dies.

I called Jane to let her know that Peter was dead. I assumed by then she'd be in the cocoon of a car with her cousin moving forward on a highway. But she was still waiting on a street corner for her ride, standing in the rain. Had so little time really passed?

The nurse came back into the room. I asked if she could close Peter's mouth before Jane saw him. The nurse was young and said she didn't think so, and I quickly said not to bother. I couldn't stand the thought of any more of Peter being broken.

"Where do you want the body to go?" she asked. *The body, the body.* But, of course, that was what stretched out before me now, just a shell of the man I love.

"I don't know. I hadn't thought of it."

I got up and went to speak to my town friends, A and H, who had arrived at the hospital. I told them Peter had died. They hugged me but there was no comforting me then. "Can you do something practical for me?" I asked. "Find me a funeral home where I can send Peter's body. I don't want him left in the morgue overnight."

Before Jane arrived, A had an answer for me; a local funeral home would transport the body there and meet with me the next morning. I walked in and out of the room where Peter lay. I made calls to family and friends, talking while I stared at his unlined face. If I couldn't have his voice in the room, I needed to fill it with mine. Anything but the deadly silence. Again, I wondered if he heard me speak. Again, I wondered how I managed to say the words *Peter has died* so calmly when they were the harshest words in the world.

When the nurse told me Jane had arrived, I walked down the narrow corridor, which seemed longer and narrower than it had before, as if it were closing in on me. Jane and I held each other tight in the waiting room, not speaking for moments, oblivious to the people waiting in chairs around us for whatever emergency had brought them there that night.

I explained to Jane how Peter looked. "Are you sure you want to see him that way?"

"Yes." She was tougher than I thought, determined to look at the man who had been an inspirational father to her, one who had fostered her love of reading and writing, kindled her imagination. We went back to the room and looked at Peter as if we were both trying to store one more image of him. But she didn't cry. She was in the same movie as I was.

I wanted to believe that some essence of Peter was still in the room, that he could see that Jane had come to say goodbye. He had loved her so, had wanted to be the best parent he could. One night in his first year with us, he had made her sit at the table and finish the broccoli that was growing cold on her plate. As she sat there determined not to eat the broccoli, he realized he didn't want to be the kind of authoritarian father he'd known. Later, when we all moved in together, he'd taken a parenting course offered at the school to make sure he did the job right. He had, and Jane knew it and loved him for it.

Jane and I lingered in the hospital, waiting for the death certificate to be signed by the doctor so the funeral home could come. It was only when staff told me the process would take a lot longer and that Peter would have to go to the morgue anyway until transportation came that Jane and I decided it was time to go home.

We left with A and H and walked to the parking lot in the dark, and in the rain that had started when I'd been in the closed world of the emergency wing. I don't remember moving my body, taking the steps to reach the car, but Jane says I muttered the word *Jesus* as if the shock slipped off me for a moment and I saw the horror of what had happened and what lay ahead. When we got back to the house, I didn't want Jane and me to go in alone. My friends came in and helped me move the furniture pushed aside by the paramedics back in place. Then we sat on the deck drinking wine and Scotch. I drank from a bottle of Scotch Peter had given me. He loved to tell the story of how I came to favour the spirit. I had been writing a scene one Saturday morning in which a man was enjoying his last Scotch before going to prison, but I didn't know what Scotch tasted like. I'd found a small bottle in our liquor collection and tasted it. Tasted it and liked it. Since then Peter had spoiled me with bottles of the finest single-malt Scotch, which I often drank while he enjoyed a grappa. We had done that the evening before on the deck to mark one month of marriage.

The four of us sat now under the canopy that sheltered the deck while a soft rain fell. The solar lights cast their small beams of light, refusing to reveal much more than the contours of the garden. The trees at the back were black skeletons in the waxing moon. Under the earth, vegetable roots were silently spreading; above ground, tomatoes and red peppers were turning minerals and water into growth. I didn't know if I could ever look at that garden again, ever forgive it for going on after Peter's heart had stopped.

Chapter Fourteen

IN THE DAYS THAT FOLLOWED Peter's death, it was not just the garden that I couldn't forgive. I hated every nuance of change that took me farther from Peter. I hated that I kept eating meals he wasn't there for, hated that I had conversations I couldn't tell him about, hated that there was news in the world he wouldn't hear. I hated the ads on Netflix that told me the new season of *Longmire*, a program he'd been waiting for, would start soon. Without him as a viewer. Without him in his chair and me trying not to fall asleep on the couch in the great room. I hated that my hair got dirty and was growing infinitesimally longer by the hour.

It wasn't just that I wanted time to stop; I wanted it to go back to a moment when I could have changed something, anything that would have kept him alive. Anger was my fuel in those days. Disbelief my functioning mode.

If he couldn't be with me, I wanted to be dead.

In a state of unawareness, I plucked tomatoes and greens from my Victory Garden, ate them without much attention. Other than collecting its harvest, I paid the garden little heed. Its abundance was a rebuke. *Victory* now seemed the stupidest of words. I couldn't bear to think what a fool, what a fucking idiot I'd been to believe I could control anything.

I'd completely ignored the most basic lessons the garden had been trying to teach me the entire season: things fail, nothing lasts forever.

In those days, Jane found some comfort in what she saw as signs. She tells me it rained the morning after Peter's death as I sat under our canopy on the deck making more calls. I remember nothing but greyness all around me. She says Peter sent the rain for the garden and that when I stood up to walk inside the house, he stopped the rain. But I was too rational for signs. I knew only that Peter wasn't there with me, and my head was too full of ratty thoughts to see any signs even if they were there. Regrets and recriminations took up too much room in my brain. Over and over and over and over I relived that last hour of Peter's life. Why hadn't I asked him what was going on? Why hadn't I found out why he didn't want to lie down on the stretcher? When I wasn't reliving that hour, I was reliving that day. Had he known he was dying? Had he read something in my writing that had made him give up? Had he waited for me to come home? Oh, why had I gone away for even a few hours? I relived the weeks before his death when he was having acute troubles with his digestive system. Should I have stepped in and forced him to go to the hospital? Could he have suffered some sort of perforation that led to septic shock and his heart failure? I relived his year with cancer. What if doctors had caught it earlier? What if we'd kept the same doctor in Toronto, who knew him so well? What if the surgeon had been certain he'd got all the cancer?

On the surface, I must have sounded and looked stunned, but the people I spoke to on the phone and encountered in person seemed to believe I was coping. When I told a friend I felt empty inside, she seemed surprised. "But you're handling things so well."

It was at the funeral home the morning after Peter died that I first sensed how my outward manner bore no resemblance to my shattered, hollow interior. From the moment I walked in the door of the old house that was now divided into rooms for mourners and offices, I knew I wanted to spend as little time as I could there. It was a place of death, after all, and I couldn't accept that Peter belonged there or could possibly have any connection to its fussy furniture and the finality of its cushioned silence. Yet the young woman Jane and I met seemed to think me capable of making decisions that I didn't want to make or couldn't accept needed making. She smiled and spoke in soothing tones, but I didn't believe she understood what I was going through.

I had steeled myself, though, and was insistent that Peter had requested a cremation and that was all I was looking for. Eleven years earlier, when we'd stood on a ghat on the Ganges River in Varanasi, India, we had watched the smoke from the cremation pyres swirl into the air and we had both agreed it seemed an appropriate way to let a body go, so much so that each of us had put our wishes for cremation in our wills.

Death had been all around us that day by the Ganges. Peter and I had got lost finding our way to that sacred river; we had followed narrow laneway after narrow laneway until we finally came to a wide opening that led to a platform and steps to the river. Touts instantly surrounded us and we knew we had to move one way or another to try to lose them. We agreed to go to the left toward the funeral pyres, since we couldn't see what lay ahead the other way. It was a fateful decision. If we had turned right, we would have walked into a tea cart that exploded about the time we would have passed it. The explosion killed seven people that day and wounded many more. Even turned away from the explosion, we felt heat and a movement like a shove on our backs before we heard the echoing boom.

It was as though we'd escaped death that day, and I kept a postcard of the ghat on a small bulletin board by our side door in Toronto so that each time I left the house I was reminded that we were alive. Peter had escaped death so many times, survived so many operations and illnesses, that part of me had believed he would never die.

But there I was arranging his cremation as though I were someone else, with my broken self floating above me. In a firm voice, I told the young woman I'd handle the memorial service and the death notice myself. She then outlined the package I'd have to buy to get the cremation, and although she said, with a smile that looked coy to me, that she didn't want to push anything more on me, she kept suggesting ways the funeral home could help: with the catering, with a guest book, or with the thank-you cards they sold, for example. Then she took Jane and me to the showroom to look at their selection of coffins and urns, even though I'd already told her I wanted the simplest of both. In the showroom, there was a necklace on display and when I asked why there was jewellery there, she said it could be filled with the ashes of a loved one, an idea that was both repugnant and ghoulish to me. I wanted to share that detail with Peter, to have him say how ridiculous it was. I wanted more than anything to hear his laugh. Every oddity, every new bit of information on cremations, every cost, I wanted to tell Peter about. Why were they making me decide all these things when every single decision was another step taking him away from me? I hated that he wasn't there to make these decisions with me.

As we sat across from the young woman, Jane sensed that I was growing more and more infuriated. As the woman spoke about all the forms and all the official letters they would take care of and those I'd have to handle myself, Jane pulled out a notebook and proceeded to make lists. She wrote so furiously I think she intimidated the woman and I loved her a little more for that.

When it came time to sign the form for the cremation, the woman showed us where we could check a box if we wanted to keep any metal parts from Peter's body.

"Some people make art from them," she told us.

We all found that a peculiar thing to do, but I did remember that, when he'd had his orthopedic surgery four years earlier, Peter had wanted to retrieve the silver plate that had held his leg to his pelvis for most of his life. The surgeon hadn't been able to remove the plate because bone had grown over it, and he had built the new hip around the plate before adding three inches of titanium to Peter's femur to make his left leg even with the right. Jane recalled that she found some comfort looking at the titanium screw from her paternal grandmother's hip after she had died and thought she'd like to look at all the parts that had held Peter together and made him straight. If we didn't check the box, the crematorium would take all the metal and apparently sell it for charity, something Jane thought we could do ourselves after we'd seen it. So, I checked the box.

The next day — I think it was the next day, but it might have been that afternoon — we were called back to the funeral home for a "private viewing." I'd had to take their simplest package to get the cremation that was all I really wanted. The package included a service of preparing the body for the showing before the cremation. The memory of Peter's face yellowed and smoothed in the emergency room was the only one I wanted of his body. But Jane and I went into a small room where his body lay in the box; his face, with his jaw now closed, looked otherwise as it had the night of his death. I noticed the summer shirt he'd been wearing was not bunched up around his neck anymore and I pulled down the thin blanket they had covering him. I gasped when I saw they had dressed his body in a hospital gown. How he would have hated that. He hated everything about hospitals and the many times he'd been in them. He once described how just lying on a bed in an examining room staring at the ubiquitous white ceiling tiles brought back memories of counting the holes in each tile in each hospital room he'd been in. I didn't look at the ceiling in that room and knew, at least, that he wouldn't either. I was angry at myself that I had not thought to offer fresh clothes, angry at the funeral home for not asking me for some, and I wanted to leave that room as soon as I could. But for the first time I was grateful that Peter couldn't witness any of this. Such a puny mercy.

Just when I thought I had everything arranged, the woman from the funeral home called on the day Peter was to be cremated to tell us the crematorium didn't return metal parts anymore. Jane was furious. It was the same woman, after all, who'd offered us the choice of checking off the box and had put the idea into our heads, and now that she'd discovered the rules had changed and the funeral home's form was out of date, she acted as though it didn't matter.

I watched Jane as she angrily phoned the funeral home back, phoned the crematorium, then phoned the funeral home director. Her rage grew with each call as she was stonewalled with the reply that returning the metal parts couldn't be done anymore. When the receptionist at the crematorium finally told her that no exceptions could be made without the manager and he wouldn't be back before the scheduled time for the cremation, Jane swore and the receptionist hung up.

"Jane," I said to her, "you can't swear at people. You won't get anything done that way. Sometimes we have to let things go. Maybe you should let this go." I had no energy for the argument but I recognized that Jane was channelling her anger over Peter's death onto a series of bureaucrats. A few bureaucrats at utilities and banks had already met my wrath.

She accepted that she shouldn't have spoken the way she did but wouldn't accept the outcome. Once again, she took to the phone to call all the same people, this time with a polite voice, and, in the end, got confirmation that any metals that didn't melt in the fire would be returned to us. We wondered if the silver would melt, but agreed we had to let that question go.

A week or so later, when I picked up the urn of Peter's ashes, there was a box that I was told contained the metal parts. As the young woman at the funeral home handed them to me, she raised her eyebrows in a complicit way at how insistent Jane had been. I just stared at her. The woman may have been trained in the ways of handling arrangements, but she appeared to have no understanding of what grief can do to a person. After all that, though, the urn of ashes and the box of metal parts remained in a cupboard; we were incapable of making any decisions on what to do with the ashes and had no heart to open the box yet.

Jane also became fixated on the moment Peter had died. She questioned me about my memory of that evening, but time had stood still for me after I'd made the call for an ambulance sometime after seven. I had no concept of minutes or hours passing. So Jane took to the phone again, tracking down which department in the hospital would have that record. She got her answer. Peter had died at 8:35 p.m. It was only when she told me the time that I realized how fast everything had happened, from the time the ambulance had come, to our arrival at the hospital, until I held Peter's hand while he died.

Time didn't mean much the first week after his death either. Days dawned. It was rainy or it was sunny in the garden. Nights came earlier as we slipped into fall, I guess. But nights did come and they were the hardest. On the first one, on the night of Peter's death, I avoided our bedroom. Jane and I lay in the twin beds in the guest room downstairs, but I can't say we slept.

After my sister arrived the next day, I let her sleep in that room with Jane and I climbed up to the bedroom I'd shared with Peter.

I took my usual side of the bed and left his pillows and his wedge on his side. In the night, I tried to pretend he was in the bed beside me. "Rub my back," he seemed to say. And I stretched out a hand and rubbed the corner of the pillow, imagining it was his back under his white undershirt.

I slept little that whole first week. I couldn't read and, although I wanted to, I couldn't weep. There's a French expression I've always admired, *passer la nuit blanche*, which means spending the night without the blackness of sleep. But my nights were not white. They were just filled with a heavier shade of grey than the days.

And yet I found solace where I could: from Jane's efforts to cross out items on the to-do lists in her notebook. She worked frantically to notify organizations and businesses; to go through Peter's email to see what bills needed to be paid; to cancel his many magazine subscriptions and our apartment in Rome, which we thought Peter had done; to turn Peter's Facebook page into a memorial site. She did it all, not just to keep busy but to take the burden from me. And I loved her even more for that. I also took solace from my sister's presence. She nurtured us both with dinners out and kindness. And I took solace from the calls, the emails, and the responses to my post on Facebook about Peter's death. Peter had been admired and loved by many. And although that was cold comfort, it was comfort of a sort.

And yes, despite my anger, I found comfort in the garden, in the silence of the yard, in the trees that swayed in the wind, in the flowers I could gather any morning I wanted. And with the colours of the vegetables in their last burst of vitality. Throughout it all I ate: restaurant meals and salads from the garden, tomatoes, eggs with basil each morning. Grief didn't put me off my food. I still couldn't bring myself to work in the garden, but it gave me all I needed. My Victory Garden became my nurturing garden, although I wasn't particularly grateful for it. I felt that my body, with its continued need for good food, betrayed my need to hang on to despair.

Somehow, in my fog, I came to conclusions about how to honour Peter. I didn't want to ask for donations to the Canadian Cancer Society; I didn't want cancer to be his legacy. Instead, I chose two places in town that Peter had been supporting as a volunteer. On the day after Peter's death, I had to call the librarian in town because Peter was scheduled to be the host at their first Wine and Words event the following week. In our conversation, I said I'd heard that the library had been used for memorials in the past and she said they'd be honoured to offer their space. So the library, soon to undergo a renovation, seemed like a good spot for donations.

Then, the next day, as I was putting out the garbage, a man Peter worked with on a committee for the new park in town stopped his car and got out to speak to me. And I remembered how much Peter had wanted to keep up his work, for as long as he could, to make the park a reality. Although Peter had never been a gardener himself, he was particularly excited at working with an Indigenous group as it developed the healing garden they wanted to include on the lands. As the man offered his condolences, I came up with an idea and blurted it out. Could the committee set up a fund so that friends and family could donate to it for trees in Peter's name in the new park? He said he'd be glad to arrange it, and although I'd done it all through happenstance, I felt like I'd found two appropriate ways to honour Peter: through books and trees.

I was, of course, making everything up as I went. Beyond cremation, we had never talked about what would happen when one of us died. I couldn't help wondering if I should have broached the subject. If on that day on the deck after we'd learned of the second, inoperable tumour, I should have said to him, "I will do what you want to fight this but if you want to talk about your feelings of death at any time, then I am here for that, too."

I never got to say that to him and Peter gave no indication he wanted to talk about death or what he wanted to happen after he was gone. Justice Ruth Bader Ginsburg of the United States Supreme Court once shared the advice that her mother-in-law gave her on her wedding day: "In every good marriage, it helps sometimes to be a little deaf." But I always found that it helped to be a little mute. It was something I'd developed in those early years of our relationship as I witnessed his gnawing physical pain and quickly learned it was wisest to bite my tongue until later, when the pain might ease and he would be open to listening to my gripes or suggestions. And during our year of cancer, I'd learned to keep many of my fears and negative thoughts to myself because he was so determined to remain optimistic.

Remembering those truths about us helped me. I slowly began to forgive myself for making decisions about his legacy without his input. And then, even more slowly, began to forgive myself for not asking more questions on the night he died. Even in that crisis, the old pattern of waiting to talk to him later when he was calmer came into play. And, at some level, I felt grateful that I hadn't probed and caused an angry reaction that night. We hadn't spoken any meaningful words in the last half hour of his consciousness, but we hadn't said any words that we could never take back.

September thirteenth wasn't a Friday that year — it was a Tuesday — but it had all the hallmarks of that unlucky day. It started out like another in a row of days of getting things done. Jane and I had one more visit to the funeral home in the morning, this time with a male representative. I liked the man's manner because he didn't try to pretend he knew our grief. Still, the visit with him shook me. As we sat at a table in the room filled with the sample coffins, urns, and death souvenirs, he slowly cancelled Peter's life — the handicapped sticker we had for the car; Peter's passport with its stamps from Argentina, U.S. Department of Homeland

Security, Heathrow, Frankfurt, and Madrid; his government iden-
tifications — and pulled out a document that would protect Peter's
identity now that he no longer had one. I signed letter after letter
to government agencies; the man quickly added a death certificate
to each letter and stuffed the envelopes. As Jane watched him lick
each envelope shut, she asked him if he'd ever seen the *Seinfeld*
episode where poison in envelope glue kills George's fiancée. He
had seen it, and he laughed a little. It was strange how a joke about
death in a funeral home could lighten our mood. Then Jane went
to the bank with me, where a kind agent tried to make sense of
Peter's accounts.

But later that day, while trying to see what monies Peter
owed, I discovered he hadn't paid his taxes for the past year. I
remembered clearly, or so I thought, the details of a conversation
we'd had in the spring; we had each prepared our tax information
for our own accountants and we were dropping them off one
day in April when we were in Toronto. But neither the Canada
Revenue Agency nor his accountant had any record of Peter's filed
taxes. And that wasn't a one-off. Around that time Air Canada
sent me an itinerary change for the flights to Rome that Peter
told me he had cancelled. Again, I remembered the conversation;
he'd said that the money from Air Canada was going back onto
his credit card.

Meanwhile, a friend who was checking our voice recorder for
the wedding vows Peter and I had recorded told me there was no
such file. I remembered sitting on our sofa recording those vows a
week after our wedding, when I'd suggested it.

"Why?" Peter had asked suspiciously then.

"So we'll have them," I said, "to listen to on our anniversaries."

And when I phoned Peter's Juravinski team to ask why they
hadn't phoned back about his digestive problems, they said he'd
never called. I began to wonder if I'd gone crazy and imagined all

those discussions. Every possible scenario left me distraught and sent me farther from any sense of reality, farther from him. But I did know I wasn't insane. Two days after the day he died, Jane and I searched through Peter's iPad for the outline of the thriller he'd said he was working on and would send to us at the end of the week. We both remembered his words. But there was no outline to be found. It appeared he'd never started it.

That evening, after I dropped Jane off at the bus to go back to Toronto, I drove to nearby Niagara College for one of the two photography courses I'd signed up for to keep my mind occupied through another fall of treatments. After Peter died, I had thought of dropping the courses, but decided I'd need some structure over the next few months. I sat in the fluorescent-lit room feeling exposed, pretending to listen to the instructor while, inwardly, I railed against Peter for the confusing loose ends.

At home, I poured two very fat fingers' worth of Scotch and started going through papers in his office. There's a reason that sleep-deprived surgeons shouldn't operate and sleep-deprived pilots shouldn't fly. And I'm quite sure — now — that sleep-deprived new widows (*Was I really a widow?*) shouldn't try to put affairs in order at midnight with a glass of Scotch. I searched that office like a crazed woman. I found a cheque from CBC for free-lance work two years earlier that he'd never cashed. And under a pile of mail, the tax information held together with a paper clip and ready to go to the accountant. The sight of it brought me some relief. Peter had prepared the information, at least. All I had to do was get it to the accountant. But I still shook with anger. Why hadn't he done the things he said he'd done? Had he always been like that and just said what I wanted to hear? Had he not bothered to hit record when we'd done our vows, even though he was an experienced broadcaster? Had the cancer fogged his brain long before we knew it was back?

I missed him more than ever at that moment. Because I wanted to shout those questions. I wanted answers and I would never get them. I remembered how Peter had said the cancer treatments were harder on me than on him and how I'd never believed it. But that night I felt that getting on with life might just be harder than dying. Like I said, not enough sleep and too much Scotch. And loneliness, gut-twisting loneliness. A toxic emotional cocktail.

Among the small unpleasant discoveries I made that night and over the next weeks as I sorted papers and received mail back from governments and employers, there were also some pleasant surprises, like cards he'd bought for future birthdays, Easters, and Valentine's Days, that restored my sense of Peter as a generous, considerate partner. One day, perhaps after some sleep, I saw Peter's iPad on his desk and remembered he had recorded the vows on it, not on the recorder we often used for interviews. I quickly found them and was flooded with comfort when I heard his booming voice speak of his love. I wanted to apologize for doubting him. In his emails, I found a link he'd sent himself on the day he died about writing letters to loved ones before it was too late. And then, in a corner of his crowded bookshelves, I found an opened package from Amazon. It was Leonard Cohen's newest CD (and ultimately his last), *You Want It Darker*. Peter and I had listened to his penultimate album, *Popular Problems*, on our winter drives to the Juravinski. We both found the maturity and sense of mortality in that album touched something in us, and I became more of a Cohen fan than I ever had been, repeatedly listening to every version of "Hallelujah" I could find on YouTube. I knew Peter had left the package there to give me on my birthday the following month. But I immediately played the CD, finding the end-of-life tones both haunted me and connected me to Peter in a way I hadn't felt in days.

I came to know that I would never have answers to all the questions I had, but that my sense of Peter would hold, that someday my memories would leap back over that horrible time to all the good memories of travel, home, and the love we'd shared.

Around the time I was struggling with all that, I got my first sign. And it was in the garden. Earlier that summer, Peter had said he'd like another Japanese maple tree. I'd planted a small one that a neighbour had started from a slip and offered me after Peter died. I went out one afternoon to take some photos of the tree before it dropped its now vibrantly red leaves. I stopped first to harvest tomatoes and green beans for my supper and then stood by the black raspberry bush I'd planted in the spring for Peter, and I ate its first bittersweet fruit. Then I photographed the maple tree in the glorious light of the slowly setting sun. As I walked beside the flower beds looking for other shots, a butterfly landed near me on the pink flowers of a sedum, a butterfly I'd never seen before in the garden. Its wings were a purply brown with iridescent blue dots at the edge before a yellow border. It stayed on the sedum with its wings open long enough for me to get a good close-up shot. Inside, I searched for the butterfly in Google Images and discovered with a gasp that it was called the mourning cloak butterfly. I still didn't have Jane's faith in signs, but it comforted me nonetheless. It made me feel closer to Peter than I'd been able to feel as I took care of his finances and made sense of bills. It made me look around for him.

The next day, I decided I had to get back to the garden. The Victory Garden had become a mess. Weeds had taken advantage of my neglect and run rampant between the rows. Tomatoes had rotted on the vine. Green beans had grown too long and too tough for eating. I cultivated the rows, picked all the produce I could, but without my usual glee.

Carrying my bounty into the house I played Leonard Cohen followed by Peter's favourites, Bob Dylan and Bruce Springsteen. I listened to their familiar songs while I cooked batches of tomato sauce and tomato soup for the freezer. I suppose it was all soothing, but I still felt like I was putting on an act, as if I were responding to the old wartime beat of "carry on" because that's all I could do. That's all anyone can do.

I still had no idea how I could ever stand to be on this earth without Peter. I could go through the motions for years to come: tend to my garden, feed myself, shower when I needed to. But where was the victory in that? Where was the victory without Peter? When we'd driven back from Hamilton less than a month earlier, on the day we received the news the cancer was back, and he'd told me this diagnosis should not stop my Victory Garden project, what the hell had he meant? Did he hope he'd be there with me, or did he mean I would have to find my own victory without him? Or did he just know I'd find some peace digging in the dirt? Of all the questions I wanted to ask him, this is what I wanted to ask him most: *How can I ever feel victorious again?* What the hell had he meant?

Chapter Fifteen

GRIEF BECAME MY GARDEN. I had to tend it. Dig through the morass of my emotions to find something to hold on to. Take the time to learn grief's needs and its rhythms before I'd ever be able to create some sort of unimaginable new life that would allow me to bear my loss and survive without Peter. Trouble was, I had no idea how to go about feeling anything but hopeless.

Just as I had studied the vocabularies of gardening and then cancer, I now had to study the vocabulary of grief to find my way through it.

Broken-hearted. Heartbroken. I wondered in the first weeks if I would fall over and die. I missed Peter so much it hurt physically whenever it struck me he was gone, as it did on the day an alert popped up on my iPad screen saying Bob Dylan had won the Nobel Prize in Literature and I started to call out the news from bed to an empty house, news I knew he'd love to hear. I know it's possible to die from a broken heart. *Broken-heart syndrome,* or *takotsubo cardiomyopathy,* describes a ballooning in one of the heart's chambers following sudden and strong stress. It usually reverses itself in days, except in rare cases when it brings on sudden death. I know it's possible to die of a broken heart because years earlier I'd witnessed it happen. One week I saw a couple from Grimsby, friends of my parents, enjoying themselves at a party; the next week the husband died suddenly and was followed days later by his seemingly healthy wife. When I didn't fall dead, I wondered if I'd loved Peter enough. The only reason I was grateful to be alive in the early days was to spare Jane more pain.

Inconsolable, bereft, despairing. Those were the words of my first month. The only tools I had against them were action, distraction, and the consolation of a few people. I took care of Peter's taxes, dealt with pensions and banks, fought with the bureaucracies of credit card and phone companies. The details were endless and, while I cursed them, they occupied my mind, as dull as it was.

Then the celebration of life I was planning for Peter filled the void for a time. I listened to his CDs, picking the softer songs of his favourite rock music for a playlist to fill the library as people arrived. And I went through the thousands of photographs I had on my computer, in albums, and in boxes of our life together and of Peter's childhood, before choosing some for a memory stick I'd give to my sister, who would print them and organize them on large boards for each side of the podium the library would set up for speakers.

While I listened to Peter's music on my computer, I often found my eyes darting to the new photograph of him I had on my desk. It was taken at our wedding, at the end of the ceremony, when he was tired. But he looks relaxed and happy staring with a smirk at the friend photographing him. Hearing the songs that Peter listened to for decades, staring into his wise blue eyes, kept me close to him and dangerously allowed me to hold on to the illusion he would be back soon.

Rituals. The rituals of mourning did nothing to ease my pain. Even as I planned Peter's celebration of life I knew I was doing it to give those who cared about him a space to pay respect. It couldn't matter to Peter now and gave me a feeling of closing the door on him. When Jane lent me a copy of *A Grief Observed* by the Christian thinker C.S. Lewis, a short book he'd written hurriedly in four notebooks after his wife had died of cancer, I found my inchoate feelings about rituals pinpointed in his articulate phrasing. "All that (sometimes lifelong) ritual of sorrow — visiting graves, keeping anniversaries, leaving the empty bedroom exactly as 'the departed' used to keep it ..." he wrote, "— this was like mummification. It made the dead far more dead.... Something very primitive may be at work here. To keep the dead thoroughly dead, to make sure that they won't come sidling back among the living."

Thankfully, Lewis pointed a way forward without ritual. "I will turn to her as often as possible in gladness. I will even salute her with a laugh. The less I mourn her the nearer I seem to her."

I wanted to get there even if it would take me a long time. And when Lewis wrote that "passionate grief does not link us with the dead but cuts us off from them," I took heart that someday the joyful memories of the life Peter and I shared would supersede the harsh memories of his illness and the night he died and he would come back into my dreams as his old self.

Closure. It was another word that made me squirm. And sometimes scream in anger. As if there would be some magic moment when everything would be all right, when my grief would be solved. Presto. It would never be all right.

Spiral. Valley. These were the words travellers through grief used to describe the geography of their suffering. I already knew there would be no straight road through my profound grief, that it would be a bumpy, twisting, hilly trail with the ground beneath my feet always shifting. I knew even before Peter died that the stages of grief described decades ago were bogus. Even the word *stages* made it sound like grief involved going into one sterile room marked *Despair*, where you'd stay for a while before closing the door on that room and stepping next door into *Anger*, and finally exiting through *Acceptance*. But there were no prescribed stages; grief is a stomach-heaving, roller-coaster ride no one wants to be on. Somewhere I read or heard that the stronger the love, the stronger the grief. But I didn't know whether to take comfort in the love I'd had or lament the grief I'd face.

There were days, when I was cooking a meal or sautéing leeks or a mixture of other bright-coloured vegetables from the garden, or when I was walking through the woods by the river, or getting the house in order, that I felt I was standing on level ground with grief nothing more than a buzzing sound in my brain. Those days, I'd go to bed satisfied with my progress up the spiral, only to wake the next day as if the previous day had never happened.

The trigger for the slide downward could be anything from adding one fewer scoop of coffee to the French press than I'd done when Peter was alive or seeing a couple go into the post office together. Each activity I'd shared with Peter, each place we'd been, had the potential to send me to the bottom again. And then the buzzing would become a roar. My chest would feel crushed as though it were in the iron vice on my father's old workbench, with someone turning the handle tighter and tighter on my heart and my breath. My stomach would feel achingly empty as if no amount of food would satisfy the hollowness. The memory of Peter's touch or his voice could make me shake with longing. What I wouldn't have given on those days to be able to do the most banal of things with Peter, stopping for a grilled sandwich at a local diner, even driving back and forth to the Juravinski Cancer Centre. To yell, "Yo, Pete. You wanna whooping?"

Alone in the car, I felt his absence. He'd never got that licence, never been able to share driving duties on a long trip. But Peter had been the navigator, the guy who changed the music on the CD player, the passenger who entertained me with stories so I wouldn't get tired. After we had come back from India, we joked he was my "water walla," who would hand me my bottle of water whenever I got thirsty. Driving alone, without Peter, especially at night, made me feel all roads ahead would be lonely ones every time I got in the car. One time, driving back from Toronto in the dark, I imagined his hand resting on my thigh to comfort me.

Wallow. Just as the books I consulted reminded me grief would take time and would never disappear completely, they cautioned me not to wallow in it. Not to get stuck in the mud of grief. A line I read on Facebook echoed this: "You either get better or you get bitter." At one level, I resented the pressure to find something good out of this great loss. But at another level I recognized a truth about myself: when I'm down, I let myself feel alone and abandoned, like the child left behind the fence. And I knew that prolonging my grief could become an excuse that would allow me to roll in the mud of the melancholic side of my personality, to go through my life feeling sorry for myself. *Nobody likes me. Everybody hates me. Going to the garden to eat worms.*

I didn't want to become bitter. For one thing, Peter would never have wanted that for me. Together, we had made sure we each reached out from the dark corners of our souls. And while grief was exhausting and working through it the hardest thing I'd faced, I knew that if I stayed too long there, I would become bitter and find myself in a more exhausting, destructive state. I tried to keep the image of the Victory Garden created out of a bomb crater in Second World War Britain in mind. If I could avoid wallowing in grief, it was possible I might discover some form of self-creation out of the destruction of our joined life. I told myself that. Believing it seemed a long way off, though. I was still too angry. And wanted to shout *Fuck off* to any person or any poster that suggested I should just get on with it, get better.

Strangely, one of the books that helped me most with the idea of creating a new life step by step was *The Martian*. At CBC, I had written and produced several television pieces on space exploration. And while I wasn't a scientist, I was always energized by the excited big brains at the Jet Propulsion Lab in Pasadena, California, and other NASA facilities I visited around the States. Working on the research and scripts for those pieces made me comfortable with both the technology and the can-do attitude of the astronaut stranded on Mars in the novel. What I didn't expect from the book, which I read as nothing more than a distraction, was to feel I had to become like the character, Mark Watney. Alone and almost certain of failure and death, he never gave up. I couldn't either. The recriminations, the self-pity would do nothing but hold me back. I could not wallow.

Coping. I was good at that, but sometimes wished I wasn't. Maybe then I would have fallen and others would have picked me up instead of telling me how strong I was. I continued to eat from the garden, making sure I had all my meals in a day and there were fruits and vegetables on all my plates. I tried to set a bedtime for myself to get back into the rhythm of a night's sleep, but soon came to realize a full night's sleep would take a very long time to achieve.

When the first holiday of the season came around, I coped by avoiding it. Peter had always roasted the turkey for Thanksgiving and made the mashed potatoes to go with the pumpkin pie I baked from fresh pumpkin. No one in my family was hosting a Thanksgiving dinner that year and I couldn't bear the idea of cooking all that food at home for just Jane and me. The Drake Hotel in Toronto offered a turkey dinner, so I booked two seats.

The day after I received my confirmation, one of the Drake's employees phoned me. "I'm sorry, but you missed the deadline for the Thanksgiving special. But we'd be happy to seat you and you can order off the regular menu."

"Fine," I said. But after I hung up, I fumed. *Why did they confirm my reservation then?*

I phoned the woman back and I begged. "Look," I said, "my husband just died and I want to give my daughter and me a Thanksgiving dinner away from home."

I hadn't pulled the widow card before, but it did work. The young woman said she'd see what she could do and the next day called to say they could seat us for the Thanksgiving special.

I stayed in Toronto with Jane that weekend; we dressed up and sat at the bar before dinner. The meal was so unlike any other Thanksgiving I'd ever had and I was so grateful to the Drake for bending the rules for me and that we had a pleasant few hours. And I learned that one way to cope with holidays was to find a way to celebrate them in a way Peter and I hadn't.

Widow. How I loathed that word. It made me feel as though I would shrivel up, that I would always be an outcast from the world of couples and functioning adults. It whispered to me of deep loneliness and uselessness. But it's a word that also stirred some needed spirit in me. Whenever anyone tries to typecast me, I fight back. A woman I know told me a story about three of her childhood friends who were now widows. The first one had turned to a couple she knew for solace and then "stolen" the husband. The second one, who'd had a difficult relationship with an authoritative husband, spent all her days in anger. The third one happily continued to ask her husband for his advice three years after his death. I suppose she imagined his responses, and I wondered what that would be like. I knew I didn't want to be any of those widows, especially the first two. I'd have to learn to take on the word in my own terms, but I'd never come to like it.

There were other words that tantalized me with their possibilities: *transformation, acceptance.* But they were a long way off. In mid-October, I held Peter's memorial, and in the days leading up to it I focused on little but the preparations. I wanted it to be a celebration of all that Peter had done despite his physical challenges and of all the love and kindness he'd shown so many. My sister was busy printing the photos and a program. The staff at the library had arranged for a liquor licence and would set up chairs after the library closed for the day. I bought wine and hired a local caterer, a young woman who ran a small café in the community centre whom I knew Peter would want to support. I asked friends to speak on key areas of Peter's life and a local actor to read from Peter's memoir, *The Man Who Learned to Walk Three Times*. I wrote a tribute to Peter's optimism, romanticism, and kindness.

On the evenings before the ceremony, Jane and I walked the town practising the tributes we would both read aloud so we wouldn't break down when we delivered them at the podium. The beauty of Jane's words and the honesty of her voice stunned me.

Wonder
at the world.
Be in awe of it.
It is your mission to learn everything you can. Make
connections between seemingly unrelated things. Use
this to help people, to express yourself.
If complaining isn't going to fix the problem, don't complain.
If something reminds you of someone, send that note,
that link, that article.
Remember people.
Help them reach their goals.

Have the strength to be EXACTLY
who you are.
Play the hand that you're dealt.

Never begrudge others their happiness.

Jane's final words reminded me of how much she'd lost too, how important Peter had been to her.

Throw yourself
into life.
Even when it's scary or uncertain.
Take that leap.

If everything goes wrong and you only have a handful of
things left that make you happy: be grateful for them.
Revel in them.

Be kind to people.

Never give up.

Cherish your loved ones.
These are the lessons Petey taught us.
This is how he made the world a better place every day
that he lived
and this is how
we will honour him,
every day after.

On the morning of the service, I wandered the garden in my pyjamas, cutting flowers for two arrangements for the library, and I felt the slightest twinge of gratitude for the selection of blooms I still had. The first flowers I chose for a glass vase were the lavender-coloured roses I'd planted for Peter. He'd loved all shades of blue and purple and I'd created a bed of those colours for him. I'd bought the bush rose, called Poseidon, at the local rose grower's. It was only later I realized the roses were also called Novalis after a German poet and were a symbol of love and yearning. With the roses, I stuck in purple flowers from the butterfly bush, springy gaura, and some of the small, perfect toad lilies that bloom so late in the season. In a bigger pot, I arranged twigs, sedum, orange roses, and orange hibiscus with variegated euonymus around the base.

The day of the celebration was beautiful, sunny and warm, one of those fall days when you think summer will just go on and on. Later, the local paper reported that more than one hundred people came to the event, but I didn't count. When Jane and I stood at the podium together and spoke our tributes, with less faltering than we feared, I could see all sorts of familiar faces from our past: relatives from both sides, friends from our days at the CBC, old friends from the United States and around the province, and new friends from town and our new writing lives. But I didn't get a chance to talk to them all, to thank them for coming.

Later, some joined Jane and me at a local Irish pub. Even though Peter hadn't been able to drink beer for months, I chose the pub because for most of his adult life he'd enjoyed downing a Guinness at a table with friends.

It was a Saturday night and a crush of drinkers had taken over the dining area to listen to the live music. Friends and family crowded into a corner room I'd reserved and spilled out around the bar, raising their voices to be heard. For the first hour, I felt nestled in the tight circle of people from our lives. At one point, though, I stood alone with Jane and realized I couldn't stay on my feet any longer, couldn't say another word. I looked at those around me who were talking animatedly, making new acquaintances and renewing old friendships, and recognized that the evening would bring closure for some. They would miss Peter and talk about him fondly, but their lives were not crushed as mine was; they would not feel the loss for the rest of their lives. Jane and I said goodbye and slipped out to the quiet, dark street, leaving the noise and the party behind.

At the ceremony, one of Peter's brothers had said he felt as though part of him had died. I hadn't said anything so dramatic and wondered if that was true for me. But as Jane and I walked to the car, I started to think that more than a part of me had died. When I was in school, I hated mathematics and begged my parents to allow me to drop it as a subject after grade ten. But there was one thing I loved studying, and that was Venn diagrams. The idea of two circles overlapping to show what they shared was so visual it made sense to me. Besides, you could colour them. I realized my relationship with Peter was a Venn diagram. We had come together as adults with our own interests and the ability to function independently. Our love of Jane, our home, travel, food, art, and music (some music) and our drive to share a life of creativity, love, and respect formed the central overlap of our circles. We both wandered to the edges of our circles to our separate fascinations, knowing the centre was there and would always give our lives meaning. In my mind's eye, the overlap in our Venn diagram became a red that grew deeper and wider over the years. It wasn't a part of me that had died with Peter, but the very centre of my existence.

Inconsolable, bereft, despairing.

It was only after that night that the finality of Peter's death began to poke through my armour. And I was finally able to weep. I'd had one long cry already, one evening when I felt angry that he wasn't there. It was early in October and it came courtesy of Bell Canada. After Peter's death, when Jane and I'd made calls to arrange for all the household bills to come to me, Bell Canada had insisted they couldn't just change the name of the payer on our internet service. I had to make an appointment to have the old line taken out, the modem taken away, a new line brought into the house, a new modem and a new service started. Which I arranged. But the new service didn't work as well as the old one. And one Saturday night it stopped completely.

It happened on the same day Jane started her walk from Toronto to Niagara-on-the-Lake. No matter what I said, I hadn't been able to dissuade her from the journey. Perhaps, I thought, she'd watched the movie *Wild*, in which a young woman hikes the Pacific Crest Trail to deal with her grief, one too many times. All she would say was that she wanted to walk from her home to mine and nothing would stop her. When Jane was a child, I'd realized with both pride and alarm that she had no fear of me. She had always been determined to follow her own path. Now, I had to accept that this walk was how she wanted to confront her grief. And I had to accept how much she missed her daily contact with Peter. When Jane left home, it was Peter who texted her every day because I didn't want to be the pestering mother.

"She's alive," he'd tell me when he got a text back from her.

For a long time, he sent her alliterative greetings like "Have a whimsical Wednesday," "Have a morally malleable Monday," or "Have a scintillating Saturday," and she answered back with her own alliteration: "Have a sideways Sunday." When the alliterative ideas dried up, they switched to facts each day before going back to the daily greetings. He never forgot to text her a greeting except on the day he got his second diagnosis and the day he died.

At least I was able to convince Jane to take someone with her on the walk; she'd be travelling along some sketchy stretches of highway where drivers might harass a lone young female and she agreed it would be wise to be with someone else. She enlisted an ex-boyfriend to accompany her and promised they'd stop in Hamilton for the night, sixty kilometres from Toronto and almost halfway. Throughout the day, she'd turned on her phone from time to time to send texts of their locations. But by evening those texts had stopped.

While I waited, I called Bell to deal with the internet. I was on the phone with them for two hours, passed from one level of technicians to another. Each time I had to repeat the details. "Yes, the modem is plugged into the wall. Yes, I know what light should be flashing." They all heard the anger in my voice and the disdain I felt for a company without compassion, even though I knew the poor sods on the other end weren't responsible for company policy. While I was on hold, I couldn't call Jane; my panic grew. *If something happens to Jane,* I told myself, *I will just give up.* Finally, the last technician promised to send a service worker the next day to deal with the problem.

When I hung up I started to cry, a rasping angry cry that brought no relief. "Why aren't you here?" I yelled at the picture of Peter on my desk. "You should be here to deal with this. You always deal with this." But he just smirked back at me.

Then I got Jane on the phone and couldn't keep the frantic worry from my voice. It was almost eleven o'clock.

"We're fifteen minutes away from the hotel," she said calmly. "I'll call you when we're there."

But when they got to the hotel, it was full and the receptionist couldn't find any other rooms in the city for them. Jane called to say she was taking them back to Toronto in an Uber. She was disappointed but not upset that they wouldn't continue; her ex-boyfriend's feet were such a mess he couldn't have done another day, anyway. She knew they had to call it quits even though she believed she could have done the second day's walk. I offered to pick them up, but she refused. "I'm an adult," she reminded me, not for the first time that day. And I realized that walk might also have been her way of showing it. Her form of victory. Later, I volunteered to join her on the second half of the walk but not until spring and only if we divided the rest of the journey into two days. She accepted that idea.

It was November before my grief cracked wide open and the real weeping began. On the first weekend of the month, I drove to

Muskoka to an amazing cottage that belongs to a friend of mine from my writers' group. Each year, she holds a weekend writing retreat there and each year, I wait for that weekend with huge anticipation.

Among the first to arrive, I claimed a beautiful room with a desk and its own bathroom, and I stayed there much of the time and wrote when I could. I hadn't written anything other than notes since Peter's death, but I made myself sit at the desk with its framed vista of coloured trees and blue waters and work through the events of the day Peter died. Later, as our group sat around the dinner table and talked about what movie we'd watch that evening, I grew intensely sad. I begged off the movie, saying I probably wouldn't be able to stay awake, and walked quickly down a long hall to my room, trying to keep the sobs in. In my room, I fell on the bed and wept. I had a bath and wept. Got in bed and wept.

The next day, I wrote more and went down to the dock by myself to take pictures for a photography assignment. I felt worn out, but in some ways relieved that I was finally grieving. As I drove home alone, I felt a little scared of the long winter ahead. Since the shorter days depressed me every year, I couldn't imagine what they would do to me that year.

Peter, in his knowing, had always realized how low my mood went in those months when there wasn't enough colour in the garden, not enough green in the trees to feed me. When the dirt was too frozen for me to get my hands into it to plant seeds. When there were no vegetables or flowers to pick. In preparing for his celebration of life, I had sorted through a thick file of the cards, letters, and poems he'd written to me over the years and I'd chosen one card, dated November 1995, to read aloud at the podium. On the front was a photograph of a back road curving through birch trees with yellowed leaves. Inside, he'd written, "Dear Deborah, I know that this time of year gets you down but I wanted to give you a small reminder that spring and summer are just ahead. Be calm. Light, colour and warmth will be yours again. Love, Peter."

Light, colour, and *warmth.* They felt like foreign concepts as autumn days grew shorter. But the card reminded me again that Peter would not want me to be miserable, that he, more than anyone, would want me joyful again.

Transformation. Acceptance. They, too, felt like strangers. But at least now they were words I wanted to stretch toward, just as I wanted to be alive for the first warm day of spring and the first sign of new red leaves budding on Peter's maple trees.

Chapter Sixteen

GRIEF BECAME *MY* GARDEN. Over the next month (and during the long winter that followed) when I needed the most attention, I heard little or nothing from many of the people who had come to pay their respects at Peter's memorial. The words the surgeon had used to describe the surgery that cut out half of Peter's esophagus, *routine but complicated*, seemed to echo in my grief. No one can escape grief; it is as routine as night and day. And yet, after the rituals of funerals and sympathy cards, few know how to face the complicated pain of the bereaved or seem to want to be around it. Perhaps, I thought, people felt I had to reach out first (I couldn't); perhaps they thought I needed time alone (I did and I didn't). Perhaps they didn't know what to say ("I'm sorry for your loss" and "I'm thinking of you" go a long way).

I tried to ignore the hurt, to feel gratitude toward the good things in my life and toward those who did reach out. There was Jane, of course. There was my sister, who called me every week; an old friend who arranged a dinner of women for my birthday. There was my writing group; my new friends in town, H and A, who invited me to movies, dinners, checked on me often. There was a long-time friend of Peter's, a woman he was writing a dramatic script with, who took me on. Soon after Peter's death, she drove from Toronto and treated me to an elegant lunch, where we laughed and cried over stories of the man we both loved in different ways. Later, she heard what I'd said at the memorial about getting low in November and promised to come down again that month. She did and continued to schedule visits with me. There were A and D, who invited me to New York. Gestures large and small meant much to me that fall.

But nothing could save me from the hours I spent alone most days and every night. There was no escaping the loss and the loneliness in the still hours. And the growing fear that loneliness would be my companion for life.

To keep busy in the waking hours, I kept up my volunteer work with the committee to support a Syrian refugee family. Our original family had never made it out of Turkey, but we learned a new family with full clearance would arrive within months. I joined two book clubs in town to meet new women. I agreed to take Peter's place on the board for the new park in town in the spring. But it was a book my dear friend O sent me, called *Grieving Mindfully*, that got me truly thinking that although I had to keep up social connections, it was up to me to dig my own way through my grief. No one else could do it.

One day when Jane was feeling particularly sad, she wrote a letter to Peter and then wrote herself an imagined response filled with the kind of advice he would have given her. *Hey, kid*, it began, using the code word they'd chosen more than two decades earlier. I couldn't go as far as Jane, imagining his responses, but I began writing letters to Peter and often walked around the house talking to him. Perhaps, after all, I would become like the third widow of my friend's story, who kept herself happy through conversations with her dead husband. But it remained impossible to ever think I'd have a two-sided conversation since the only dreams I had of

Peter were of me abandoning him and him abandoning me. But just writing to him about my day, voicing words I'd spoken so often to him, brought me some relief. And sometimes, I could almost imagine his response because I knew so well what he would say to me in so many situations. Whenever I walked out on the deck and left the screen door open, I could almost hear him holler, "Close the door!"

Around the same time, I knew I had to make some changes in the house to shake me into realizing my life had changed forever. I bagged all of Peter's clothes except his beloved blue suede shoes Jane had bought for him after his leg surgery, when he could finally wear regular shoes again; his favourite ties with Venetian lions and books on them; some sweaters I thought I could wear around the house; his black leather jacket; and his housecoat, which I wrapped tightly around me each morning. Then I took the green garbage bags of clothes — many of them new pieces he'd bought in the summer for his shrunken size — to a local charity that donates clothes to migrant workers. When I got back home, I claimed both closets in the bedroom for my own clothes and set up the bed for one person with two pillows in the middle.

Each morning, though, when I came down the seven steps from our bedroom to the main floor, I was faced with Peter's office as he'd left it. Just as seeing Peter at his desk reading or writing on his computer had been my first happy view of the downstairs most mornings for the first two years in our house, the empty desk was now the first sad thing I saw before making my first cup of coffee.

When a local handyman came over to do some fixes in late fall, I had him and his partner move the desk up to my bedroom and move down a club chair that sat in the corner of the bedroom. It was the chair where Peter had slept when he couldn't stand to lie in bed on his wedge one minute longer and it too brought painful memories.

The new arrangement in the bedroom worked. The previous owners had turned two small bedrooms into one large one with windows that looked out both the front and the back of the house. Our bedroom furniture took up one half of the room. The other end of the room had been filled with the chair and a dresser with a glass-fronted cupboard on top of it. I was relieved to see the desk didn't overwhelm the room. Rather, it looked instantly like it belonged there. I'd had the men turn the desk so the now empty space for books faced the window and I looked each night at an unfamiliar side with drawers that Peter must have seen each day. The desk became a new place to write thank-you notes and letters to Peter beneath the window that overlooked the street, a view I'd never had. Those little shifts in perspective set off a little shift inside me to become someone who could live alone in her bedroom retreat and feel safe there while still connected to a shared life that was now gone.

To bring Peter into the room even more, I went down to the basement and found the boxes marked "Owls." For years, Peter had collected glass, stone, and wood owls whenever we travelled. And when I was away for work in countries he'd never get to, I brought home handcrafted owls as gifts. In our old house, the owls had sat randomly on his bookshelves. Sometimes, he'd move them about, have them face the books or the window. But he hadn't opened the boxes of owls in the new house. He'd wanted to keep his new office orderly, and he'd managed that as well as any man could who brought new books into the house almost daily.

When we'd moved to our new house, our goal had been to keep it as uncluttered as possible, the opposite of our Toronto house, which had always felt cramped and full of objects we didn't really need. We'd kept only the furniture from our old house that worked and bought new pieces that fit our style and space. Although I loved the new house even after Peter died, I had an uneasy feeling that since we'd set it up for years to come, I had somehow jinxed us. I'd had the same feeling after my first marriage ended and I was left in a house we'd bought as the home we'd stay in. Our "death house," my ex had jokingly called it. If I moved again, I told myself, I'd try not to care so much about the dwelling, try not to think of it as a permanent home.

After we'd arranged the new house to suit us, I'd always meant to find a spot for Peter's owls. The day of the furniture shift, with Peter's desk beneath the bedroom window, I pulled the books we collected for immediate reading out of the glass-fronted cupboard and lined up the owls on the shelves. Whenever I walked by that cupboard after that day or reached for something in the drawers of the dresser below it, I remembered — or tried to remember — where each owl had come from.

It was harder to find a new balance in Peter's office, which had been his domain since we'd moved into the house, the first room I'd painted and set up. My town friend A moved Peter's computer that, without a desk, sat on the floor into my office and configured it as a storage server for my thousands of digital photographs.

But I had to decide what to do with all the books Peter had accumulated. Before we'd moved out of our Toronto house, he had got rid of thousands of books. As he'd packed up the ones he wanted to move, he mumbled a phrase I thought I'd never hear: "There is such a thing as too many books."

As well as the shelves in his office, we'd lined the family room in our lowest level with more bookshelves so he could control the number of books in his office. Still, after less than two years in the house, books sat in second layers on shelves and piled high in the corner units.

As I reorganized the office, I pulled all the books off the shelves, organized them by category on the floor, and over two weeks decided which ones to put back on the shelves, which ones to move downstairs, and which ones to give away. There were volumes and volumes on subjects I'd never want to delve into: Pope Pius, euthanasia, and arcane histories. Peter had more books by and about Sherlock Holmes than I'd ever known he had or would ever know what to do with. Some of them looked rare. I kept the collected stories of Sherlock Holmes with the profile of the detective and his pipe across the bindings. I put it back on the centre shelf because I still wanted to remember Peter when I came down the stairs each morning, but in a gentler way than the empty desk allowed.

In the end, the room reflected both Peter's taste in books and my minimalist style and it felt like a library. It still needed more seating, but I'd get to that someday. Without planning to, I had also made the room my personal museum. On one shelf, all I put was the album I'd made of our wedding and the wood backgammon board Peter and I had played on most days. In one corner unit I placed copies of Peter's books with some of his favourite boxes and souvenirs. He'd bought a stone at the United States Holocaust Memorial Museum in Washington, D.C., with the word *remember* carved into it. I set it near his books.

As I straightened the backgammon board on its shelf, I wondered if I'd ever play the game again. I had no desire to touch the board, which I'd bought on a work trip and we'd played on for more than twenty years. It felt sad to try to play both sides of the game on it and too sacred to use with anyone else. But I didn't want to forget how to play the game Peter had taught me so many years ago, so I decided I'd play matches on his iPad, which we had used as a travel board for the past few years. And maybe if I played both sides, Peter would win more often.

Peter had downloaded a game to his iPad and set his identity as Owlreal. I didn't quite understand the name; perhaps he'd had to search for some variation of *owl* that hadn't been used. He'd listed me as Deborah DeMarco. It was a name we'd come up with after watching the 1995 movie *Don Juan DeMarco*, in which a delusional character believes he is "Don Juan, the greatest lover in the world." After that movie, Peter took to calling me "Deborah DeMarco, the greatest backgammon player in the world."

The morning after the room was finished, I read the paper on the green chair while I drank my coffee. I admired the room's re-creation but I also felt miserable knowing it wasn't Peter's office anymore. The charge: betrayal. The verdict: guilty. It would take some time for me to be truly comfortable with the room as a library in my home and not just a pretty room I'd set up like a stage.

With those tasks done, I tried to get on with our seasonal routines. I couldn't imagine anything ever having the sense of purpose or fun it had when Peter was around, but after I read the paper that morning, I got out the bird feeders we hung each winter on the frame for our summer canopy. As I filled the feeders, I kept thinking Peter would like what I was doing, as though he would be coming back to see the birds fly through the yard to eat there. Later, when scarlet male cardinals came, resting in trees on one side of the yard before flitting to trees on the other side, Jane saw them as another sign. Cardinals were about male energy, she said, and Peter had sent them. I couldn't let myself believe that, and I suspect she didn't really either, but I liked that she was finding comfort in the signs, and I smiled, despite myself, whenever cardinals flew through the yard after that.

Through the fall I puttered in the garden. A year and half earlier a reporter from the local paper had come to interview Peter about his memoir. She'd written that I was "puttering" in the garden while they talked on the deck. I'd found the word dismissive then, but now it seemed to appropriately describe my movements. I moved through the garden with little attention to what I was doing. I still resented it so for surviving. But at least the work wasn't too taxing; I'd done it all before.

November was a tender month. Unusually so. Jane might have said that Peter had sent me sunny, surprisingly warm days to help me get through the toughest November I'd had. I didn't have to think about the weather as I worked. It was never too cold to make me want to rush into the house for a cup of tea or pile on more layers of clothing. If Peter wanted to send me any gift, weather that I could just be in was the best one.

When I finally turned my attention to getting the vegetable beds ready for winter, I left the rows of kale and spinach. If the winter wasn't too harsh, they might survive until spring. But I dug out the remaining beets, carrots, and onions, picked the remaining butternut squash off the vines, pulled out all the tomato plants. From plants lying on their side, I separated the beans into two piles on the lawn: beans I could eat or freeze and beans I'd keep for seeds. In the back of my mind, I wondered if I would bother planting beans the next spring. I couldn't imagine the vegetable patch now lying barren before me as a second Victory Garden. Still, in the spirit of going through the motions, I pulled out weeds, spaded the vegetable beds loosely, and laid bags of manure.

In the rest of the garden, I cut down all the sedum as I'd learned to do the first year in the house, trimmed perennials, piled soil around the rose bush crowns, and began watering the roots of trees before the freeze up. Those jobs seemed more practical. If I decided to leave this house the next spring, I'd want the garden looking its best before a sale.

But I had no idea if I wanted to stay in the house that had been Peter's final home or move somewhere else. Even then, I knew I couldn't escape the loneliness of life without him just by changing residences.

I had no heart for plotting my vegetable beds for the next year, although I needed to figure out a new spot to plant the garlic. It was time. Had it just been a year since I'd last set cloves in the soil with so much fear and hope? I lacked both the energy and the faith to start drawing maps with well-spaced rows and the promise of perfect vegetables for a season that seemed impossibly far off. In the end, I decided the easiest plan was to plant my garlic cloves at the other end of the smaller bed where I'd planted them the year before and worry about the larger vegetable patch later.

As I carried out the garlic I'd grown in my Victory Garden, I told myself I was just doing a job on a list. I reminded myself that grief, like writing or keeping a garden, is step by step, clove by clove. Besides, if I were alive the next year, I'd still have to eat. But as I knelt on the ground, some of the old magic came back. Not a thrill, exactly, like I was birthing new plants or anything that profound. But a spark of faith that the cloves I was dropping into the soil would survive buried in the darkness; that once again they would slowly transform into fat roots and healthy shoots. They were programmed to do that. But what would my change be over the winter? There was no program I knew of that preordained what the darkness of grief would do to me.

Before I could put the whole yard to bed, I had to get all the furniture and hoses into the shed. I put away the garden Buddha, the top of a small fountain Peter and I had bought the year before for the soothing sound of water. I put away the chairs, the orange cushions, and the tables. Each job took me farther from Peter's last summer in the garden, erasing his presence from the yard. Each object I set on a shelf or in a corner of the shed increased my doubt of making it through the winter to another spring when I'd see them again.

The sun was getting low in the sky on that November afternoon. Without the sunshine, a chill was settling into my bones. With cold hands, I filled the watering can to complete my work for the day by watering the freshly planted garlic so the earth would compact around those cloves and hold them tight. As I stood in the peace of our yard, listening for the songs of birds and a single voice that had disappeared, I knew that somewhere inside me I had, like the inner knowledge of the garlic clove, a will to push myself into the light again.

After my separation in my thirties, when I thought I'd never have much of a life beyond caring for Jane, I had blossomed. And preferred the person I became, the partner I became with Peter, a man who saw me as I was. But this was different, I told myself. I had no desire to blossom or even come to accept Peter's death. I couldn't shake off my feelings that to thrive was to betray him, to give up on his memory. The garden had no clear answers for me that fall day; all it could do was allow me the quiet and the space to jump from despair to hope to despair.

The one task that gave me true pleasure in my last week in the garden was spreading my compost from a summer's worth of food and yard waste. When I opened the bins, I didn't have to fake the joy I felt at all the new soil I'd created. I threw bucket after bucket of it over the vegetable beds, breathing in its sweet aroma, running my hands through its soft richness. I knew the compost would ameliorate my soil and provide a home for soil microbes, so vital to my crops. But my joy was more than the satisfaction of a vegetable gardener building a healthy plot of land. I couldn't put my finger on what I was feeling until later, when I read some research that claimed that mere contact with *Mycobacterium vaccae*, found in soil, releases serotonin in the brain. I wondered if long ago, when I'd dug in the dirt as a toddler waiting by a gate, I'd made that discovery myself. I know that dirt always makes me happier, gives me resilience to face life when the odds are against me. I think Peter knew it, too. Sometimes my hands would be so covered in dirt, I'd approach him on the deck with a kissy face and hands raised as though I might rub them through his hair and over his face. He never flinched. He always just smiled.

From despair to hope to despair to hope. Perhaps, just perhaps, in the coming spring, in my garden, on my knees, I might find some bliss again as my fingers dug in the dirt and my jeans grew muddier. And my vegetables grew. Perhaps my cancer wartime Victory Garden would become a garden of my own self-preservation.

The happiness fresh produce gave me never really disappeared that fall, even if I couldn't taste all its flavours. But without greens and squash from my garden, pasta smothered with my tomato sauce with a side kale salad, a bowl of neon red-pepper soup, I would have felt emptier — both in body and in soul. When I didn't have enough vegetables from my gardens left, I drove to Lococo's Fruits and Vegetables in Niagara Falls, a grocery store started by an Italian immigrant 110 years earlier. The store was not much more than a warehouse with three large rooms. The last room housed meats, fish, and prepared food, but I rarely stepped in there. From the first two rooms, I'd fill my cart with lettuces, berries, snow peas, and cabbages. On one day tomatoes would be cheap, on another day red peppers. I loved throwing extra peppers into my cart, surrounded by shoppers filling bag after bag with the plump red jewels at a bargain price.

As a treat, I'd buy myself a passion fruit imported from Colombia. When Peter and I had gone to Vietnam, we'd both been enthralled by the tiny fruit cut in half and served to us first thing at breakfast. We'd hunted for them in Toronto and occasionally found them. And there they were in Lococo's, each small ball wrapped in plastic for just under a toonie. If I bought a passion fruit on a Saturday, I'd cut it open on Sunday, place the two halves in a small bowl and ceremoniously eat the fruit at the dining-room table, remembering long Sunday brunches Peter and I shared there and the breakfast room in Vietnam where we'd first tasted the fruit. Eating passion fruit offered an exercise in gratitude and mindfulness. It doesn't take long to scoop the yellow seeds tinged with purple from the two half orbs, and it's easy to eat them before you're aware you've finished. But I made myself lift the spoon slowly and leave the seeds on my tongue while the tart sweetness filled my mouth.

Just as with dirt, science supports my instinct that fruits and vegetables make me happier. Before he died, Peter had emailed me some research from the University of Warwick that showed "happiness benefits were detected for each extra daily portion of fruit and vegetables up to eight portions per day." I knew dirt and vegetables would both be strong allies on my road through grief.

But, of course, there wasn't enough dirt or vegetables in the universe to fill the hole in my heart. And no November could ever be gentle enough to lull me into thinking winter wasn't coming. Besides, events that month seemed to intensify the chaos in me. The great Canadian songwriter Leonard Cohen, who'd been suffering with cancer, fell and died, one of many celebrities who left the earth in 2016. *What did they all know?* And as I drove along a country road after my photography class on November eighth, the black skies seemed to deepen with the news that Donald Trump would become the next president of the United States, news I couldn't digest and dissect with Peter. It was as though I were in the cracked universe of Cohen. I've never felt as lonely as I did driving in the only car on Concession 7 Road that night listening to the sombre voices of Michael Enright and Susan Bonner on a CBC radio special. It was going to be a long, lonely, and now disturbing winter.

Later, on my trip to New York, I wandered through one of the shops Peter loved there, the Strand Book Store. He was first drawn to it by its motto: "18 miles of books." I wouldn't buy any books that day, only a calendar with trees to remind me of Peter every day in the new year and a button that read "Fuck 2016." In the liberal shops of New York, the button referred to Trump's election and all the havoc he might wreak. For me it was far more personal.

As late November frost settled on the roof of the house, all the bleakest questions from the days after Peter's death returned to freeze my heart, threatening to block the new cracks in my grief. *What could we have done differently? Why did this happen? If I'd loved Peter more, put him before me, would he still be alive?*

But then I noticed a change in tone to the questions: *What will I do? What will I become? How can I keep Peter's memory alive and allow new things, new people to come into my life? How will I become self-reliant and find concrete ways to work through my grief? What would the Martian do?*

My guilt that Peter was dead and I was *not* still stuck in my throat like food in a cancerous esophagus. But I couldn't deny that the energy of life coursed through my body. That there was light pushing its way into the cracks, that the resilience I found by playing in the dirt surrounded by trees would get me through. And I came to believe that this was the victory Peter had urged me to find.

Just before November ended, I found a Vesey's seed catalogue for 2017 in my mailbox. At first, I thought of throwing it out; its shiny, colourful pages reminded me too much of the foolish hope I'd placed in creating a Victory Garden a year earlier. But, instead, I left it on a stool in the kitchen. The next morning, as I sipped my coffee and the sun rose higher behind the bare trees at the back of the yard, washing the kitchen with a warm, shadowy light, I picked up the catalogue. *Just a quick peek*, I told myself. *I'm not ready to order anything. I probably won't get any seeds this year.* But by the time I began to flip through the alphabet of vegetables and arrived at beets, I was hooked. Slowly, I stood up to get a pen from my office. And then I began to circle my choices.

Acknowledgements

MY DEEPEST THANKS to everyone at Dundurn Press, especially Kathryn Lane and Rachel Spence for their enthusiastic response to my submission, and to Allison Hirst, Laura Boyle, Heather McLeod, and Elena Radic for their work on this book. Beyond Dundurn, thank you to Arun Kapur for the author's photo and Susan Fitzgerald.

I first wrote this as I lived it, relying on meticulous notes I took after each medical appointment, gardening step, and situation I found myself in. Along the way, I was encouraged by early readers Olenka Demianchuk and Nita Pronovost, and supported — as always — by my amazing writers' group: Maria Cioni, Maria Coletta McLean, Janet Looker, Shelley Saywell, Barbara Tran, and Jamie Zeppa. I'm grateful for Hedgebrook's Master Class in Goa, India, in 2018, where fellow writers and instructor Elmaz Abinader treated sections of my work with kindness. Elmaz's insistence that I "drill down" helped me immensely with my rewrite.

Digging through research is almost as much fun as digging in the soil. I spent hours at the Toronto Reference Library reading wartime newspapers and garden books. In the New York

Public Library, I pored over old how-to booklets and the proceed-ings of National Victory Gardens Conferences. Of all the books I consulted, three helped me the most: Cecilia Gowdy-Wygant's comprehensive *Cultivating Victory: The Women's Land Army and the Victory Garden Movement*, Twigs Way's *The Wartime Garden: Digging for Victory*, and the online reproduction of Charles Lathrop Pack's 1919 book, *The War Garden Victorious*. Mine is by no means a scholarly work, but I sought multiple sources and tested my knowledge on the head gardener at the Smithsonian Institution in Washington, D.C., as he planted his replica Victory Garden in the spring of 2018.

Unlike a book, grief has no ending. I have leaned on friends and family and sought ways to move forward at a retreat and with a wise social worker. I am thankful for them all. Through the incred-ible services of Hospice Niagara, I have walked with the bereaved and hiked in awe-inspiring woods. I've been sustained by fellow travellers on this grief journey; no one should go through a deep loss alone.

Finally, my endless gratitude to the two people who have been my life's greatest gifts: My daughter, Jane Awde Goodwin — the kindest person I know — gave me free rein with her thoughts and words. And I am beyond thankful for the love and guidance of Peter Kavanagh, who read many of these pages with his calm, gen-erous, but firm insistence that I carry on with the project. How I wish he could hold this book, with a different ending, in his hands.

Book Credits

Acquiring Editor: Kathryn Lane

Developmental Editor: Allison Hirst

Managing Editor: Elena Radic

Editorial Assistant: Melissa Kawaguchi

Copy Editor: Susan Fitzgerald

Designer: Sophie Paas-Lang

Publicist: Saba Eitizaz

🌐 dundurn.com 📷 dundurnpress
🐦 @dundurnpress 📌 dundurnpress
📘 dundurnpress ✉ info@dundurn.com

FIND US ON NETGALLEY & GOODREADS TOO!

🏛 DUNDURN